BREAKING THE CYCLE

To Melissa,

I hope you enjoy
reading !

Love from
Luna x

BREAKING THE CYCLE

Escaping Diet Culture, embracing food freedom & inspiring change

Luisa Mannering

Cherish
EDITIONS

First published in Great Britain 2024 by Cherish Editions
Cherish Editions is a trading style of Shaw Callaghan Ltd &
Shaw Cal-laghan 23 USA, INC.

The Stanley Building, 7 Pancras Square
King's Cross
London
N1C 4AG
www.triggerhub.org

A CIP catalogue record for this book is available
upon request from the British Library
ISBN: 978-1-916920-78-1

This book is also available in the following eBook formats:
ePUB: 978-1-916920-79-8

Luisa Mannering has asserted her right under the Copyright,
Design and Patents Act 1988 to be identified as the author of this work

Cover design by More Visual
Typeset by Lapiz Digital Services

To all the adults who deserved an upbringing free from the harmful influences of diet culture, may you find peace and freedom in embracing your true self and pass this wisdom on to the children of tomorrow.

CONTENTS

CONTENTS

FOREWORD

I've often said that infants are born with instincts and emotions, but their thoughts, beliefs, and language must be taught. In my over forty-three years of working with clients to help them combat the toxicity of diet culture,

I have found that the seeds of their own beliefs originated in the messages they heard about food and their bodies in their home, at the doctor's office, in the media, or at friends' and relatives' homes.

One of the most profound warnings in the play "Into the Woods" comes from the song by Stephen Sondheim entitled, "Children Will Listen". Here are the lines:

"Careful the things you say
Children will listen
Careful the things you do
Children will see
And learn

Children may not obey
But children will listen
Children will look to you
For which way to turn
To learn what to be
Careful before you say
"Listen to me"
Children will listen"

I was so taken by these words, as they expressed what I hear from the majority of my clients who come to me to heal their disordered eating and eating disorders. Their relationship with food and body was formed by what they either overtly or covertly heard while growing up.

In this poignant and informative book, Luisa Mannering weaves her personal story of how her lived experiences led her to a relentless fear of food and to a focus on changing her body to meet society's standards of thinness, with that of her daughter's experience of being brought up by a mother who rejected diet culture. What a contrast!

Clearly and powerfully, she explores the toxicity of diet and beauty culture and the force it holds in damaging those who are vulnerable to it. Not only do these self-serving industries promote perfectionism and unnatural thinness while bringing financial benefits to their owners, but they also damage self-trust and self-esteem. In addition, this toxicity has a powerful global impact. At this level, it leads to the oppression of those who either will not or cannot pursue and achieve these goals. Anti-fatness and weight stigma land in the same sphere and produce the same hurt as any oppression that sucks the life force out of those in marginalized identities.

Luisa begins by explaining the meaning of diet culture and all of its ramifications. She then presents how the external messages from diet culture gaslight people into believing that they are unworthy unless they strive for thinness (with the belief that this is attainable and sustainable) while depriving themselves of the joy of eating. These external messages soon morph into internal messages that occupy an overwhelming amount of mental space.

As Sondheim warned, "Children will listen". And, as you absorb this profound message, Luisa expertly leads you to understand the consequences of exposing children to diet culture. But understanding is only the beginning; the book's breadth takes you through the steps that will bring healing in your relationship with food and body and help you protect your children from diet culture's destructive forces.

One of the many important messages in this book is to be patient in your process of breaking the cycle of diet culture's oppression and moving to a place of freedom and trust in eating and your body. As mentioned earlier, you were not born with the demands of diet culture. They may have taken root in early childhood, but the branches have grown and extended over many years. With self-compassion, you will be able to accept that the journey has many layers of learning and unlearning. Approaching it slowly will allow for new thought patterns to emerge and replace the negative thoughts you may have carried with you throughout your life.

Luisa also does a deep dive into body image--a topic that affects most people. She bravely presents her personal history and explores the multitudinous influences that informed her body image. And then, at last, she brings us back to childhood, exploring the role models, powerful words, and comments children experience during their formative years. With practical recommendations, focused on self-care, self-compassion, empathy, gratitude, and critical thinking, this book offers the hope that future generations will be shielded from the toxic forces that lead to negative body image, disordered eating, and lowered self-esteem.

Stories from the lived experiences of people who have been affected by diet culture show a stark difference between how they have suffered, and the gift Luisa gave to her daughter by raising her in a world that defied it. *Breaking the Cycle* presents hope—the hope that the messages that children hear as they grow will be devoid of negative body and food language. Instead, they will hear and experience positive role models who speak of the satisfaction and joy of eating and the focus and appreciation of a body's simple existence in the world, rather than how it looks.

Remember, every word you say about yourself, every bit of negative body image you display, and every judgmental implication you make about your child's body or the food they eat is heard and absorbed. Never forget that "children will listen"!

Elyse Resch, MS, RDN, CEDS-C, FAND
Nutrition Therapist
Co-creator of *Intuitive Eating*

INTRODUCTION

Raised in Diet Culture

Who could ever blame a child for falling into a vicious cycle of dieting, calorie counting and spending their lives locked in a daily battle with food, the scale, the mirror and their bodies?

Diet culture is everywhere: applauding, idolising and congratulating weight loss and small bodies. This messaging surrounds us all daily, seeping into every pore of our being, affecting us consciously and even subconsciously. We have been taught that a certain body type is the ideal and that we must do whatever it takes to attain it. Unless we attempt to break the generational cycle, how can we expect anything different for our children?

The COVID-19 lockdown of 2020 profoundly magnified societal views about weight gain. Fat-phobic memes and diet and exercise programmes convincing us to shrink our bodies and control our food intake were everywhere on the internet, on TV adverts and in the media. These messages were also the buzz in WhatsApp group chats and online Zoom meetings. As millions of people around the world became ill, lost their lives, their loved ones, their livelihoods and suffered numerous difficulties due to the pandemic, diet culture seized the opportunity to jump on the bandwagon. It bombarded us relentlessly with its toxic messages, making it impossible to escape the resounding demand: shed those pounds!

What is most terrifying is that our children were also exposed to this negative and disempowering messaging; they were listening, watching and learning. Our future generation was absorbing everything they saw and heard. How many little ones while stuck at home for months on end overheard their parents or caregivers frantically obsessing over weight gain, calories consumed and exercise programmes? In millions of households across the country, children were absorbing the message that only a thin body type is acceptable. They picked up that food is something that must be restricted and controlled because bodies *must stay small*.

As I observed the events unfolding during the pandemic, it brought back memories of the origins of my own preoccupations with my body and food, which began when I was a young child. Throughout my formative and teenage years, I was consumed by worries about my food choices and body size, which robbed me of precious time and experiences. It is only through extensive therapy that I have been able to find healing in these areas of my life. The idea of any other child having these precious years stolen in a similar manner is truly unbearable and is the primary motivation behind writing this book.

Why I Wrote this Book

From a young age, I absorbed the message that getting fat was the worst thing that could happen to anyone. I listened carefully as the women in my life shared their weight loss goals, swapped dieting tips and idolized thin bodies. They were constantly seeking new ways to lose a few pounds. I watched them try every fad diet under the sun in a desperate attempt to become smaller, as though their life depended on it. These funny, colourful, hardworking, amazing women dedicated their entire lives to trying to drop a dress size. They spoke candidly about their measurements and exact weight and shared their very disordered eating habits daily. So, from an early stage in life it was deeply ingrained in me that being thin was important and the only way to be.

Being thin meant being in control, disciplined, successful and desirable. In my family, being overweight was utterly unacceptable. I felt compelled to avoid gaining weight since anyone deemed as fat were subjected to mockery, ridicule and gossip. A larger body was seen as a source of shame, and signified being ugly, greedy, lacking self-control and laziness.

The 1980s – my teenage years – was a time when the pressure to be thin wasn't just limited to the influential figures in my life. It seemed to surround me from every angle. The messages ingrained in my mind were reinforced by the mothers of my friends, doctors, teachers, nurses, magazines, catalogues and newspapers that were a constant presence in my life. Even the toys I played with and the clubs I frequented echoed the same sentiment. Whether it was through TV programmes, movies or the ubiquitous advertising in supermarket aisles, shop windows and billboards, the pervasive theme was clear: thin bodies were idealized and held up as the ultimate standard of beauty.

As I entered adulthood, the bombardment of these messages intensified. Nearly every magazine I came across featured cover stories centred on diets or exercise routines, luring readers in with the promise of a dramatic "body transformation". These publications were adorned with images of models or actors showcasing what was deemed the epitome of perfection, complete with explicit details of their measurements, weight and even their daily consumption habits to attain such physiques. Moreover, celebrities who appeared to have deviated from society's narrow standards – particularly new mothers who hadn't shed their "baby weight" – were not only subjected to ridicule but were shamefully and publicly vilified.

I was relentlessly exposed to these messages from every conceivable source, leading me to internalize the notion that thinness was the sole path to finding happiness in my life. It became ingrained in my routine, and I found myself dedicating each day to obsessively monitoring my weight, engaging in excessive exercise, and restricting my food intake – all in a desperate quest to shrink my body size.

During my early twenties, I had the privilege of crossing paths with two extraordinary women who would go on to profoundly transform my life. These remarkable individuals exuded a genuine acceptance of their bodies and embraced intuitive eating as a way of life. They didn't adhere to diets or strive for a thin ideal. What struck me the most was their unwavering indifference toward societal beauty standards and their firm rejection of the mainstream media's messages. They wholeheartedly embraced and unconditionally accepted themselves just as they were. It was in those days that a lightbulb sparked within me, forever altering my perspective.

To further blow my mind, one of these incredible women gifted me a copy of *The Beauty Myth* by Naomi Wolf and that was the turning point for me. I became a convert and aspired to be just like them. I yearned to reach a point where I no longer cared about the daily fluctuations on my scale, and I craved a harmonious connection with both food and my body – something that should be the birth right of every individual. This book, an immense source of inspiration, marked the initiation of a profound and transformative journey toward healing my relationship with food and my body.

I began to unravel the beliefs that had been ingrained in me since childhood, and I couldn't help but question their validity. Had I been deceived all along? What was the true meaning behind it all? Why did I harbour a fear of food and find myself obsessively weighing myself multiple times a day? Why was I paralysed with fear at the thought of my body size being judged when wearing a swimsuit? Why did I persist in squeezing into clothes from my high-school days? Why did I approach each summer with apprehension, knowing I couldn't hide my body under big baggy sweaters? Why did I constantly strive for thinness? Why did I believe my worth was contingent on how others perceived my size? Why did I scrutinize my body in every reflection and mirror, constantly seeking validation that it wasn't too fat? Why did I meticulously count calories, embark on a new diet every Monday, and relentlessly berate myself for not resembling the women plastered across magazines and billboards?

It took an extensive and dedicated journey through specialized therapy spanning many years to gradually heal. Furthermore, over the past 25 years, I have wholeheartedly immersed myself in the exploration of this topic, meticulously documenting my experiences in countless diaries. These personal reflections have played a pivotal role in helping me comprehend the profound impact of the societal teachings ingrained in me during my formative years, which led me to believe that my body had to conform to a narrow standard of "thinness" in order to be deemed acceptable. While I may not possess formal expertise as a body image specialist or be a professional in this field, it becomes evident that the pervasive influence of diet culture, which enveloped me from birth, heavily influenced my thought processes and behaviours and led to the development of an eating disorder.

Upon completing a counselling course in 2013, I found myself presented with a fantastic opportunity. For several years, I dedicated my time as a volunteer, leading support groups for individuals who, much like me, grappled with challenges related to food, weight and body image. It struck me profoundly to learn that most service users were also raised in homes where weight was heavily emphasized, thin bodies were praised, body shaming was normalized, and food carried immense significance. These individuals also carried the weight of a legacy that perpetuated an unhealthy relationship with food and their bodies, leaving them in an ongoing, daily battle and suffering from debilitating eating disorders.

The deep impact of my volunteering experience, hearing the stories of hundreds of other people who shared strikingly similar upbringings and experiences to mine, and more recently witnessing the reality of children's experiences during the pandemic have compelled me to share what I've learned.

I can't stay quiet and do nothing. Diet culture is pervasive and entrenched in our society, especially within families, and our children are in danger unless we attempt to break the destructive generational cycle. We urgently need to intervene and initiate radical change within families to undo the detrimental impact that diet culture has had on us for generations. It's vital to protect our children from this harmful influence and prioritize their wellbeing to prevent them from going down the same path.

The goal is to be the parent or caregiver who dismantles diet culture at home or in any environment where we interact with young people. These actions are crucial in enabling our children to critically evaluate the credibility of the bombardment of information by diet culture and the beauty industry. While we may not be able to eradicate diet culture or single-handedly challenge the vast industry behind it, there are numerous steps we can take to break the cycle. We are not powerless. We possess significant influence over how our children develop their attitudes toward food and their bodies. By incorporating small changes into our own language and behaviours and teaching them empowering beliefs, we can inspire them to lead happier and more fulfilled lives.

The Claws of Diet Culture

Recent research reveals a concerning rise in body image issues and eating disorders. According to a 2022 NHS report[1], the number of young people seeking treatment for eating disorders has reached a record high. Compared to the previous year, there was a 25% increase, and it is nearly two-thirds higher than before the pandemic.

Although eating disorders are complex mental illnesses that vary from person to person and can be triggered by various factors, the lessons that children receive in their household have the potential to plant a seed that profoundly impacts their relationship with their body, possibly leading to the development of eating disorders.

Christy Harrison researches the origins of diet culture in her book *Anti-Diet*, and explains, "Diet culture is in the air that we breathe."[2] It's not our fault for thinking that our worth is determined by our body size and that being thin is necessary to be considered valuable. Throughout generations, powerful global industries have preyed on our insecurities through clever and massive marketing campaigns focused on weight loss, beauty, fashion, cosmetics and fitness. Diet culture has been ingrained in us for a long time, shaping our beliefs. The media's portrayal of unrealistic beauty standards has become deeply rooted in our minds. Since childhood, we've been taught that smaller is better. Our mothers – and their mothers before them – have desired and still desire thinness. We've grown up under constant scrutiny, internalizing the idea that having the perfect body will bring us happiness.

Impressionable Minds

While the media holds significant sway over body image, it is essential to recognize that parents and caregivers serve as the primary role models for children. In their book *Body Image in The Classroom*, Nicky Hutchison and Chris Calland assert that "children primarily shape their beliefs, attitudes, and behaviours based on the influential adults in their lives."[3] From an early age, they absorb and mimic the language and conduct of the adults around them, wholeheartedly believing and imitating their words and actions.

Our children are constantly exposed to the adults around them criticizing their own bodies and those of others. They unintentionally overhear conversations about dieting, weight loss goals, calorie counting and intense exercise regimes. Without realizing it, these discussions send a powerful message about the extreme measures taken to shed weight and the perceived importance of doing so. Children are always listening, absorbing the praise given for weight loss and the judgments passed on others' bodies. Our society places a strong emphasis on appearance, where discussions about diets, exercise and body shaming have become commonplace. People openly discuss these topics without recognizing the potential harm or long-term impact on impressionable ears.

Peggy O'Mara, author of *Natural Family Living*, astutely states, "The way we talk to our children becomes their inner voice."[4] Children are innocent, trusting, vulnerable and receptive, readily absorbing messages both consciously and subconsciously. If they are consistently exposed to adults who express dissatisfaction with their bodies, they will grow up perceiving this as the norm. Over time, these messages will inevitably influence their own self-perception.

Many of you reading this will most likely relate, having grown up listening to similar messages. How many of you were taught that smaller bodies are superior and something to strive for, while larger bodies were deemed shameful and unappealing?

A Better Future

This book isn't about blaming or shaming the adults in my life or criticizing those who believe that being thin is the key to happiness. It's about creating awareness for the sake of future generations. The focus is on understanding diet culture and how it distorts our relationship with food and our bodies. Most importantly, it's about changing the conversation at home and teaching children that all foods are acceptable, and all bodies deserve love and respect. Everyone deserves a healthy and peaceful relationship with food and their body.

Who would wish for their children to tread the same challenging path we did? To spend their childhood viewing their body as their enemy, constantly feeling like there is something wrong with it or feeling embarrassed by it? Believing they are too fat, too thin or too big, that their legs are too chunky or too skinny or that their tummy is too wobbly? To feel self-conscious in their sports kit? For them to be in a constant daily battle with food and weight?

Even the briefest contemplation of them experiencing such hardship: whether through restricting or bingeing on food, calorie counting, or excessive exercise for weight loss or to bulk up is too agonizing to bear. They deserve better – as did we. While it may be too late for us, as we gradually unlearn these ingrained beliefs, it is not too late to break this cycle for our children.

It is crucial to address the serious issue of how adults discuss food, weight and bodies in the presence of children. I often contemplate how different my life might have been if I hadn't been inundated with diet culture from a young age. Would I have been susceptible to developing an eating disorder, convinced that all my problems would be solved if I simply became thinner? I firmly believe that the messages surrounding food and bodies that I absorbed as a child had a profound impact on shaping my experiences throughout my life and destroyed years of it.

About this Book

This book aims to inspire change within families, offering a different path for our children and breaking the cycle that persists across generations. It will help you understand the consequences of being exposed to diet culture as a child and show you how to create a positive environment where children see all bodies as worthy bodies and don't view food as their enemy.

If our aim is to break the harmful cycle of yo-yo dieting, eradicate body negativity and prevent eating disorders within families, it's vital to bear the responsibility of educating ourselves on the profound impact that certain language and behaviours can have on children. We must learn to be mindful of our own actions and words – especially in the presence of children.

The initial chapters of *Breaking the Cycle* delve into the pervasive influence of diet culture and the beauty industry, exploring how they mould our belief systems and foster a societal fixation on appearance, fuelling a constant battle against our own bodies. They examine the profound impact of growing up in a diet culture, and how ingrained beliefs and distorted perceptions surrounding food and body image can profoundly and detrimentally shape the lives of children. They shed light on the phenomenon of bodies becoming mere trends, and how ideas about body image have evolved over the centuries.

In the following chapters, the book explores diet culture through the eyes of a child, exploring the perils of developing a negative body image and offering practical strategies to foster positive transformation.

In the concluding chapters, our attention turns to the power of positive role models, fostering mindful media literacy within families, enhancing overall mental wellbeing. These chapters offer clear guidance on what to do and what not to do. These insights pave the way for our collective journey of liberation, empowering children to cultivate a positive connection with food and their bodies.

Throughout the book, I weave in my own upbringing, deeply immersed in diet culture, and offer guidance based on my discoveries. My daughter graciously shares her personal journey of growing up with a mother who steadfastly rejects diet culture. I believe her story brings hope that it is possible to break this toxic cycle within families.

1

DIET CULTURE AND THE BEAUTY INDUSTRY

Understanding the power and impact of diet culture and the beauty industry is crucial for challenging its influence and fostering a healthier and more inclusive relationship with our bodies, food, and overall sense of worth. This chapter sheds light on the pervasive toxic messaging that surrounds us, constantly infiltrating our daily lives and leaving us with a perpetual sense of never feeling good enough. It explores how this detrimental messaging profoundly influences individuals, shaping their self-worth primarily around their physical appearance. This chapter asks: What exactly is "Diet Culture"? What is its overarching objective? Why do "Diet Culture" and the "Beauty Industry" wield such significant power? Why do these industries have such a profound influence on the way we navigate our lives?

Bodies as Commodities

Diet companies and the beauty industry thrive on fostering self-doubt and negativity within us. They rely on it. Our insecurities become the target of large corporations who convince us that a complete transformation of our appearance is necessary to experience genuine self-worth. These industries fabricate body "problems" to sell us the supposed solutions, all while reaping enormous profits. Their tactics are convincing and relentless, with the primary goal of cultivating repeat customers. From a young age, we are conditioned to feel a moral obligation to conform to the media's portrayal of the "perfect" body type. Additionally, we are enticed with the promise that attaining the "perfect body" and the "perfect look" will bring us happiness and solve all our problems.

We live in a society deeply fixated on appearance and image, making it almost impossible to remain unaffected by the constant stream of negative messages. Whether it's through magazines, TV shows, social media, movies or advertisements, we are bombarded with direct and indirect reminders that our bodies are inadequate. We feel inferior when we compare ourselves to the idealized images of slim, toned and tanned bodies. Falling short of these standards leaves us feeling like failures. We set unattainable goals, only to berate ourselves when we inevitably fail to meet them. We become convinced that we must alter our physical appearance to feel deserving of love and acceptance. We find ourselves in a constant battle against our own bodies. It's rare to come across a woman who is genuinely content with her appearance. The overwhelming pressure to conform to specific physical standards is all-encompassing and our bodies are reduced to mere commodities in the consumer market.

The World We Live In

Let's begin by examining the prevailing societal attitudes toward female bodies. Our environment is saturated with messages that indoctrinate us into believing that our bodies must be thin and that we must strive for the elusive ideal of a perfectly toned beach body. It is considered normal behaviour to exercise to the point of exhaustion to try to achieve it. We are also bombarded with the notion that we must look "young" and resort to any means necessary to defy the natural process of ageing. We are encouraged to undergo cosmetic procedures such as freezing our muscles, inflating our lips, enhancing our breasts, wearing hair extensions, lengthening our eyelashes, indulging in fake tans and wearing fake nails. We are bombarded with a relentless stream of information regarding "good" foods, "bad" foods, diets, healthy eating plans, wellness regimens, fat-burning techniques, cosmetic surgery options, body toning devices, calorie tracking applications, transformative exercise routines, personal trainers, weight loss and detox programmes, slimming clubs, anti-aging treatments and creams, all with the promise of a younger, thinner, leaner, more desirable, more acceptable and worthy appearance.

These influential and manipulative messages permeate our daily lives, subjecting us to immense and unwarranted pressure throughout our existence. The pervasiveness of damaging messages propagated by the diet, beauty and wellness industries has created a narrow and restrictive definition of beauty. It comes as no surprise that countless individuals find themselves caught up in relentless cycles of appearance obsession, body dissatisfaction, weight fixation, dieting and eating disorders.

How many people do you know who navigate life in a state of perpetual hunger, obsessing over every morsel consumed, desperately striving to attain a smaller body size, firmly believing that achieving the "perfect" body will bring them happiness? Week after week, they make promises to themselves that they will start afresh on Monday, vowing to be "good" from that point forward. They go through life feeling like failures as they relentlessly pursue the elusive ideal of the perfect body. They find themselves embroiled in a daily battle between food, weight, exercise, the mirror and the scale. They readily invest in fad diets, "slimming" products and any exercise regimen that promises to grant the perfect body. For numerous individuals, altering the shape and size of their bodies has become an all-consuming life mission. Hours are spent in front of the mirror, filled with self-criticism and anguish. Others willingly pour significant amounts of money into treatments aimed at modifying their body and facial features, some even resorting to surgery. The bulk of our population is immersed in the pursuit of the perfect body.

It is considered normal in our culture to discuss diets, weight loss and body size. Women often bond over self-loathing and excitedly discuss the size and shape of other women. These conversations have become so commonplace that they dominate in various settings, from casual encounters on the street to formal environments like offices, schools, yoga changing rooms and even online communication channels like WhatsApp groups. Thin bodies with sculpted physiques and tiny waists are not only admired but envied by all. We find ourselves participating in these discussions not necessarily because we want to, but often to fit in and avoid feeling out of place.

Regrettably, we often engage in these discussions without realizing the profound impact they may have on our children. Even pre-schoolers are aware of "good" and "bad" foods, while girls as young as six are grappling with appearance concerns. Shockingly, girls as young as six say they want to be thinner and eating disorders are recorded in children as young as eight.[5]

In the current landscape, diet culture is an ever-present force that subtly infiltrates nearly every aspect of our lives, often without us even realizing its presence. It's not merely confined to the covert messages in TV commercials or magazine ads; it cunningly lurks in the aisles of supermarkets, nestled within the fine print of clothing sizes, and is sneakily woven into the fabric of our social media feeds. It emerges in the worship of specific body types, the fixation on numbers – be it calorie counts or scale readings – and in the glorified narratives around extreme exercise routines. Even hunger, something our bodies naturally experience, becomes glamourized and valued as a sign of power and discipline. These facets, seemingly innocuous or normalized, collectively contribute to the insidious nature of diet culture, shaping our perceptions and behaviours in subtle yet powerful ways.

RECOGNIZING DIET CULTURE

Diet culture falls under many guises. If you are familiar with any of this language, you are familiar with diet culture:

Detox plan
Beach body
Summer body
Drop a dress size in
   10 days!
Guaranteed weight loss
   plan
Fat-burning
Fat free
Fat melting

Calorie burning
Cheat day
Clean eating
Guilty pleasure
Guilt free
Wellness plan
Transform your body!
Get beach body ready
New Healthy Eating Plan

The following comments also encompass diet culture:

- "Wow! You have lost so much weight! You look great."
- "I need to be good this week."
- "You are so lucky, you're so tiny."
- "You have so much willpower."
- "She has let herself go."
- "I wish I never ate that; I'll pay for it."
- "Those jeans are so slimming."
- "I'm wearing this to cover up the sins."
- "How do you do it? You have so much discipline."
- "Did you lose weight?"
- "You must have a good metabolism."
- "I am going to be good and order the salad."
- "Okay, I'll get a takeaway, but I really shouldn't."
- "You need to get your steps in!"
- "I'll make up for it."

Diet culture surrounds us all and has become a normal part of everyday life. It affects everyone, and we can't avoid its influence. The fear of getting fat is real. According to the University of Missouri's Centre for Body Image and Policy, 40% of people agreed that it would be worse to gain 25 pounds during quarantine, than to become infected by Covid 19.[6]

Even our children are directly targeted. Have you ever seen a flabby Barbie, fat L.O.L. doll, an "imperfect" Disney Princess or a superhero that isn't muscular and toned? The realization of what children are absorbing is terrifying. They keenly observe, picking up conscious and subconscious messages from the adults around them. Innocent, vulnerable and receptive, they emulate our words and beliefs, internalizing them as their own. Expecting them to cultivate a healthy perspective on food and weight becomes an unrealistic proposition when they are continually exposed to negative and unrealistic messages. What they are exposed to inadvertently programmes and conditions them to believe that conforming to a certain appearance is the aim in life. We will delve deeper into this topic in a subsequent chapter.

So, What Exactly is Diet Culture?

Diet culture can be understood as a pervasive system of beliefs and practices that prioritize weight loss, body size and appearance as markers of success, health and happiness. Its aim is to perpetuate the idea that certain bodies are more desirable and superior to others based on narrow beauty standards. Diet culture thrives by encouraging restrictive eating, promoting the idea that our worth is intrinsically tied to our ability to control our food intake and manipulate our bodies to fit these ideals.

It is an all-encompassing force that affects individuals regardless of age, gender, religion, culture or social status.

Many people you know are most likely engaging in diet culture, even if they are not actively on a diet. Many have succumbed to societal pressures and have internalized the need to be in a smaller body, at any cost.

Diet culture exerts immense power for various reasons. Firstly, it taps into our deeply ingrained insecurities, promising a solution to our perceived flaws and a path to acceptance. It preys on our desires for belonging, self-esteem and societal validation. Additionally, diet culture is often fuelled by industries that stand to profit enormously from our pursuit of an unattainable and ever-changing "ideal" body. This dominant cultural narrative around diets and body size is deeply entrenched in our society, perpetuated by media, advertising, and even our education and healthcare systems.

Diet culture insidiously infiltrates our subconscious through the constant exposure to negative and subliminal messages that have become an inescapable part of our daily lives. It influences the way we perceive ourselves and others, our relationships with food, our exercise choices and our self-worth. It affects our overall wellbeing – and that of our children – as the same deeply ingrained beliefs are passed down through the generations.

Rarely do we encounter plus-size mannequins in shop windows. Reality TV shows often showcase perfectly sculpted, tanned and toned bodies as the epitome of desirability. Websites and billboards display airbrushed and digitally enhanced models who appear flawless from head to toe, toned and curvy in all the right places. This false image of perfection becomes the unattainable standard to which people aspire, and the messages reinforcing it are never far away.

Even a quick trip to the supermarket reveals the latest promotions for slimming products, such as "detox tea" and "guilt-free" snacks. What does it mean to label a snack as "guilt-free"? Are we supposed to feel guilty for indulging in a snack that doesn't bear this label? At local cafés, it's not uncommon to hear someone ordering a "skinny" latte or cappuccino. The very name of these beverages implies a promise that they will contribute to weight loss.

In a profound Instagram post, Sydney-based nutritionist Monica Fenwick aptly encapsulates the essence of diet culture with her words:

"A system of beliefs that smaller equals better, healthier and deserved of more worth, oppresses those that don't fit its supposed picture of health."[7]

The underlying message that promotes small bodies permeates our lives in various disguises. It instils within us a fear of becoming "too big" and imparts the notion that we cannot trust our own bodies or appetites. Diet culture teaches us to vilify certain foods and to impose restrictions on our food intake. Implicitly, it conveys the message that our worthiness and happiness are contingent upon the size of our bodies.

Diet culture celebrates, applauds and idolizes weight loss, fostering the belief that a smaller body equates to a superior and healthier body. It persuades us that achieving a smaller body is the solution to all our problems, promising that a slim physique will lead us to a flawless existence.

Let's unravel some subtle influences, exposing diet culture's reach, to begin empowering ourselves to break free from its grip.

Diet Culture and Exercise

Within the realm of diet culture, exercise is often perceived as having a singular purpose: weight loss. It is regarded as a means with which to punish oneself for consuming calories and to compensate for food intake. Individuals invest significant time and money in adhering to exercise regimens that promise transformative body changes, often utilizing a personal trainer to maximize impact.

Megan Jayne Crabbe, author of *Body Positive Power*, astutely described exercise within the context of diet culture in an Instagram post:

> *"Diet culture teaches us that movement only exists to sculpt our bodies into something new, punish ourselves for enjoying food, or earn our next meal."*

She goes on to emphasize:

> *"Movement should be fun! And joyful! And a celebration of how we can feel in our bodies. It should never be a punishment for how our bodies look."*[8]

Crabbe's words serve as a reminder that exercise should be approached with a mindset of enjoyment, pleasure and gratitude for what our bodies can do, rather than as a means of punishment or body manipulation dictated by external beauty standards.

Until my early twenties, I perceived exercise solely through the lens of diet culture. Little did I know, it could be an enjoyable pursuit, not merely aimed at shrinking my body or burning calories.

Diet Culture's Obsession with Numbers

Diet culture places an immense emphasis on numerical measurements – including weight, dress size, calorie intake and step counts. These numbers hold such power that a morning weigh-in has the potential to dictate someone's mood for the entire day. If the number decreases, there may be a fleeting moment of happiness, but it is quickly overshadowed by persistent anxiety and an obsessive focus on maintaining that number, or lowering it further. Conversely, if the number goes up, it can trigger overwhelming feelings of failure and self-loathing.

It's astonishing to think that we allow a simple machine, which merely reflects our gravitational force in this vast universe, to wield such authority over our lives. I myself have experienced the entanglement of becoming fixated on scale numbers, understanding first-hand how easily they can dominate and dictate one's entire existence – regardless of the wonderful things that might be going on in your life.

How many individuals dedicate their days to meticulously counting every single calorie they consume? We must question whether we truly want to spend our valuable time meticulously measuring out every ounce of food we eat and logging every morsel we eat into an app. Surely our lives hold more worth than obsessing over such minute details, and there are countless more meaningful and fulfilling activities we can engage in. I often overhear conversations on how many calories certain individuals have burned as I am enjoying the blissful feeling of a post-yoga class. It takes effort to not be irritated at diet culture for sneaking into our yoga space.

The latest obsession revolves around counting steps. People now go to great lengths to log every single step they take, and if they fall short of a predetermined target, they are overcome with feelings of shame and guilt. The pursuit of reaching a specific number of steps or calories burned becomes an endless quest.

Diet culture thrives on numbers and relies on our fixation with them to sell us the latest products flooding the market. We must pause and reflect on whether our happiness and fulfilment should be dictated by arbitrary numbers. There is a whole world of experiences, connections and personal growth awaiting us, and it is crucial to free ourselves from the constraints of diet culture's numerical obsession in order to discover the true value and richness of our lives.

Diet Culture and Sizing

How frequently do we purchase clothing in a size smaller than we are, hoping to motivate ourselves to diet and achieve that smaller size? How often do individuals assign significance and power to the label on their clothing, experiencing shame and disappointment when the smaller size doesn't fit? Many people attempt to squeeze into clothing that is too small, believing that it will make them more socially acceptable, despite being fully aware that they will spend their entire day in discomfort or even agony.

The inconsistency of clothes sizing across various shops contributes significantly to body image issues in our society. With often unrealistic sizing standards, individuals find themselves grappling with feelings of inadequacy and self-doubt when they cannot fit into a certain size in one store, while easily fitting into that size elsewhere. This leads to a harmful comparison culture, where people may internalize the belief that their worth is determined by a number on a label. Such sizing discrepancies perpetuate body dissatisfaction and can negatively impact self-esteem, fostering a damaging mindset that places undue importance on conforming to arbitrary standards rather than embracing one's unique body shape and size.

It is high time for the fashion industry to adopt more inclusive and accurate sizing practices, promoting body positivity and acceptance among consumers of all shapes and sizes. In the meantime, let's focus on purchasing clothes that fit well and feel comfortable, without attaching shame to the tiny number written on the label.

Diet Culture and Hunger

Diet culture teaches us to deny ourselves of a basic human need – to disregard our own hunger signals. It portrays hunger as something negative, something to be suppressed or ignored or to be ashamed of. Appetite suppressants and various other methods are readily available to fulfil this purpose. How often have you heard someone say, "All I've had today is x, y or z", like it is some kind of massive achievement to eat only a little, like they should be rewarded for it.

Interestingly research has consistently shown that when the body is deprived of nourishment, it responds by intensifying cravings and increasing preoccupation with food. I can personally attest to this. Anyone who has dieted will tell you that what you won't allow yourself is what you obsess over and want. Denying the body of what it needs and wants often leads to a destructive cycle of restricting and bingeing, creating a turbulent relationship with food and negatively impacting mental health. In some cases, it can be the trigger for the development of an eating disorder. It is crucial to recognize the importance of honouring our body's hunger signals and nourishing ourselves adequately for optimal wellbeing. Despite what diet culture teaches us, feeling hungry a few times a day is normal, and it is possible to reach a place where one can intuitively eat again like we all once did as babies.

Feeling hungry is not something one should be ashamed of. It is interesting to think that we must be the only species to deliberately starve itself and to view it as a healthy thing to do. It is also fascinating to note that "intuitive eating" would just be called "eating" if diet culture did not exist.

Diet Culture and the Media

The media's intense scrutiny of celebrities' body size and shape is impossible to ignore. Newspapers and magazines sensationalize weight fluctuations on their front pages, bombarding us with photos of celebrity bodies. They are either unfairly criticized for minor imperfections or excessively praised for fitting an unrealistic "perfect" standard. This obsession is overwhelmingly intense, verging on madness.

When Adele, a true "national treasure", embarked on her weight loss journey, the media went into a frenzy. The "news" dominated social media for days and made the front page globally. Despite her exceptional talent, with over 120 million records sold and a multitude of prestigious awards, the media chose to focus on her body size, reducing her to a mere number. This pattern is not exclusive to Adele but extends to all female celebrities who face invasive interviews centred on their appearance, exercise routines and fashion choices, while their remarkable achievements take a backseat. The remorseless scrutiny on women's bodies is a troubling national obsession that demands serious attention and resolution.

All the above instances serve as constant reminders of the omnipresent influence of diet culture. The messages it communicates aim to create a sense of dissatisfaction with our bodies, maintaining the notion that we must constantly strive for a specific body size to be considered acceptable or desirable. It infiltrates our everyday language, our shopping choices and our perception of beauty, exerting a powerful and often detrimental impact on our relationship with ourselves, our bodies and with food.

The Beauty and Wellness Industry

The messaging we encounter from the beauty and wellness industry is as inescapable as that from the diet industry, capitalizing on our vulnerabilities at every turn. How often do you come across advertisements for creams that claim to eliminate wrinkles? How many ads and products promise to make cellulite vanish or tighten loose skin? This industry aims to persuade people that these natural features should be sources of shame.

Women are spending exorbitant amounts of money in a desperate endeavour to modify their facial features and bodies. Botox parties and regular injections have become commonplace. The latest obsession among young girls is lip fillers, while older women often showcase unnaturally swollen and expressionless faces.

How frequently do you encounter women wearing extremely large lash extensions that make it challenging for them to fully open their eyes? Incidentally, this is not meant as a judgment against those who opt for this choice; it's simply an observation of what's happening right now. Women are marketed the idea that longer lashes enhance their appearance, prompting them to invest.

The market is flooded with tanning products, all promising to give you the "perfect glow" and deceivingly suggesting that having darker skin (for Caucasian individuals) makes you more desirable. Interestingly, it's the same companies that sell skin-whitening products across Asia, using cunning marketing tactics to trick women with darker skin into thinking they need to lighten it, while simultaneously convincing women with white skin that they will be more attractive if their skin is darker.

Why can't we accept the colour of our skin the way it is? Why do we have to pay money to alter the natural colour of our skin to feel okay? It is genuinely alarming to witness what is happening right now and the lengths that women are going to alter their natural appearance.

The beauty industry promotes a plethora of creams and serums and treatments that promise miraculous solutions for our imperfect bodies: cures for wrinkles, fat melting treatments, waist trimming devices, cellulite removal, skin firming creams, slimming body wraps amongst many others. These exaggerated claims often create unrealistic expectations, leading people to invest significant amounts of money and hope in products that do not deliver the promised results. Moreover, the constant pursuit of an unattainable ideal negatively impacts self-esteem and body image, fostering feelings of inadequacy and dissatisfaction.

As a fundamental step to initiate change within our lives, we must enhance our awareness of such messaging, allowing us to make conscious decisions about how we internalize it. It is vital that we start to approach these marketing messages with a critical eye.

As consumers, we often act like puppets on a string; we are easily influenced. Regrettably, these industries prioritize financial gain over consumers' wellbeing and mental health, showing no concern for the impact on individuals. Learning to recognize these surreptitious tactics should help trigger alarm bells in our minds when confronted with such content in the future. It is important to remind ourselves that these industries solely exist to maximize profits, and we mustn't be deceived by their false promises. They attempt to instil fear, divert our focus from living fulfilling lives, and keep us preoccupied with our appearances to maintain control.

Beginning to Break the Cycle

As we move through life, we often fail to realize the pervasive influence of this "higher force" that governs our existence. Navigating a society deeply immersed in diet culture and obsessed with appearance is an overwhelming task. We can't singlehandedly change a society that idolizes and celebrates small bodies or that tells us we should alter every part of our bodies to feel worthy – however, there are many things we can put in place.

If our wish is to bring about meaningful change, we must acknowledge the overwhelming impact of manipulative messages that inundate us and our children regularly. Once we recognize the falsehoods, we gain deeper insights into their hold on us. This awareness empowers us to address the issues more confidently to help us action *Breaking the Cycle*.

Beginning to question the excessive amount of importance placed on our physical appearance is a start. We must ask ourselves if it is genuinely normal to experience guilt over a bite of food. Is it reasonable for us to subject ourselves to such harsh self-judgment based on how we look? Is it worthwhile to spend copious amounts of money and time striving to appear younger when we could be embracing the natural process of ageing? Should we be spending our entire lives waging a war against our bodies, attempting to conform to societal norms in a quest to attain acceptance and a sense of worthiness?

The next time you encounter an advertisement, magazine cover or billboard poster, make a decision to pause and reflect. When you come across an ad promoting a wrinkle cream or a fake tan product, take a moment to ask yourself: What lies behind this message? What hidden messages are being conveyed? What product is truly being sold, and who gains from it? By scrutinizing these aspects, we can develop a more profound comprehension of the marketing strategies at play and make more informed decisions as consumers with the future of our children in mind.

Would anyone wish for their child to be trapped in a harmful cycle of dieting, to feel ashamed of their natural appetites, suppress their hunger, suffer from body dissatisfaction, or spend their savings on body- and face-altering treatments, injecting their lips and foreheads with harmful substances, simply to conform and be accepted by their peers?

As we embark on the journey of trying to save ourselves and our children from this madness, we must be patient. We know that the diet and beauty industries will always be there preying on our insecurities. Unravelling this conditioning is an ongoing journey. By wholeheartedly committing to educating ourselves we can impart the understanding that genuine happiness doesn't stem from altering our physical appearance. The aim is to reach a point where we realize that it is possible to live contentedly in this world without succumbing to the pressures imposed upon us by the media and our culture. We can learn to accept ourselves the way we are and make it our responsibility to actively contribute to helping our children embrace themselves as they are.

We don't have the power to fully protect our children at all times. We may not be able to control what is said in the playground, in friends' houses or on social media, but we can be open about it, and we *can* show them that there is so much more to life than dieting, counting calories and altering our natural appearance. We can teach our children about the role these commercial giants are actively playing in all our lives and show them how they rely on us buying into their game. Only then, will our children be able to reframe the messaging for themselves.

As we reflect, it's truly striking to witness the current state of our society, where discussions around the size of a woman's body or the admiration of someone who conforms to specific standards – such as losing post-pregnancy weight – are considered captivating. For many women, struggles with body image and conversations about weight loss have unfortunately become avenues for connecting with others. This negative mindset seems to be perpetuated across generations, deeply woven into the fabric of our society.

Considering this, it's crucial for us to undertake a reflective analysis of these deeply ingrained societal norms and ponder how we've arrived at this point. It's vital to actively challenge and reform these damaging perspectives, fostering a more positive and inclusive approach to body image, self-worth and overall wellbeing. This shift is not only necessary for our own sake but for the benefit of future generations, prompting a healthier and more compassionate discourse surrounding body positivity and self-acceptance.

Hope For the Future

This chapter has shed light on the ever-present and manipulative role of the diet, beauty and wellness industries, providing you with a better understanding of their tactics so you can begin questioning and evaluating their messaging.

Initiating the journey of rejecting these messages can have a profoundly positive impact on both current and future generations. Imagine a future where our children don't fall into the same traps that many of us did. What if our children grew up with awareness, knowing that life is about more than constantly worrying about appearance, weight or altering their natural selves? And, what if we all allowed ourselves to live freely and embraced the skin we are in? Instead of battling with ourselves daily, what if we focused on celebrating the things we love about ourselves?

Our present behaviour shapes the future, as history has shown us. Body image ideals and beliefs about body shapes have changed from decade to decade, with what was once worshiped now seen as unappealing. In the next chapter, we will delve deeper into body image development and how body image ideals have evolved over the years.

2

UNDERSTANDING BODY IMAGE

If we are to effectively empower children and enhance the prospects of them leading a life with a healthy body image, it is essential that we gain an understanding of what body image entails, how it develops and its potential influence on our overall wellbeing. Enhancing a comprehension of our own body image enables us to exert a positive influence on our children and effectively serve as role models for them.

Within this chapter, we will delve into the concept of body image, aiming to gain deeper insights into the distinctions between having either a positive or a negative body image. I delve into my own personal experience with body image, prompting you to also embark on a journey of self-reflection. Additionally, we will briefly examine the evolving portrayal of the "ideal body" in the media throughout the decades and how this impacts our perception of body image. The impact of these societal norms spreads rapidly through generations, shaping the way we perceive ourselves, our bodies and how our children perceive theirs.

Learned Conditioning

To begin, it's important to emphasize that we are not born hating our bodies. In fact, from the moment of our birth, we enter the world without any judgment or criticism directed toward our physical selves at all. As we grow and gain awareness of our physical appearance – be it our size, shape, hair colour, facial features – our attitudes and emotions toward our bodies start to form. During our toddler years, we become aware of our bodies. We begin to compare ourselves to others and observe the physical appearances of those around us. As we advance in age, societal influences come to the forefront, moulding our thoughts, behaviours and responses concerning our bodies. This societal conditioning plays a pivotal role in shaping our body image and influencing our self-perception over time.

From an early age, children internalize both positive and negative beliefs about their bodies from their parents and caregivers. These beliefs are further influenced by extended family, media and programmes they consume, the influence of peers, the social groups they are part of, the toys they play with and society at large.

The current digital age daily exposes children to a vast number of images, influencing them at what is a vulnerable stage of development, leaving them susceptible to forming unhealthy and inaccurate opinions about their bodies. The prevalence of diet culture further exacerbates this issue, impacting children at a young age and potentially leading them down a harmful path of body dissatisfaction and unrealistic standards. Conversations and comments about body shape and weight, and comparisons with siblings and others both play a significant role in influencing how our children perceive their bodies and develop a body image. Over time, generational patterns related to food, weight and body image become deeply ingrained.

What Is Body Image?

Body image is often misunderstood as solely revolving around physical appearance, but it extends far beyond that narrow view. In essence, body image is primarily shaped by an individual's perception of their physical self – in simple terms, it's how one thinks one looks.

Body image actually encompasses not only how the body *looks* but also the thoughts, emotions and behaviours an individual has in relation to their body. Every aspect of a person's appearance contributes to their body image, including height, shape, weight, hair, nose and overall body size. How they think, feel and act concerning their body can lead to positive, negative or mixed feelings about the body. It's essential to recognize that one's body image is not only determined by physical attributes; it is influenced by a mental and emotional perception of the physical body.

It's crucial to keep in mind that an individual's perception of their body may differ significantly from how others perceive it. For instance, an individual may harbour negative thoughts about a particular aspect of their body, such as believing that their nose is too big; meanwhile, their friends and others might perceive it as entirely normal or even attractive. This conflict highlights the subjectivity of body image and reminds us that our own critical self-judgment may not align with how others view us. Anyone can have a positive or negative body image regardless of their physical appearance.

Body image expert Judi Craddock and author of *The Little Book of Body Confidence* describes it like this:

"Body image is part of your mental health and is your perception of your body – what you think and feel about it. Body image ISN'T what your body looks like. Anyone can have a positive or negative body image regardless of what their body looks like."[9]

Dr Laura Muhlheim, psychologist and certified eating disorder specialist describes body image as:

"Body image does not refer to one's physical appearance. It refers to the beliefs, perceptions, thoughts, feelings and actions that pertain to that appearance."[10]

We all have a body, and we all have an image of our body. Regardless of gender, religion, race or age, every one of us possesses a body, and with it comes a unique body image. Whether you are five years old or ninety-five years old you have a body image and the way you feel, see, think and behave toward your body impacts your life. For some, their body image significantly influences their daily existence, while for others, it might hold little or no importance. Understanding and acknowledging our body image can shed light on how it shapes our experiences and interactions in the world.

Let's delve a little deeper.

Main Aspects of Body Image

There are four main aspects of body image.

1. How you **see** your body – perceptual body image
2. How you **feel** about your body – affective body image
3. How you **think** about your body – cognitive body image
4. How you **behave** toward your body – behavioural body image

Perceptual Body Image

Perceptual body image is how an individual sees themselves when they look in the mirror or catches a glimpse of their reflection. It is crucial to point out that what a person sees is often distorted – others might perceive us differently. Some may fixate on body flaws that others don't even notice.

It is worth noting that the reflection that some people see in the mirror has the power to dominate their thoughts and actions for the entire day, impacting choices around food, socializing, exercise, mood and body language.

From a very young age, I saw myself as being too big and felt uncomfortable with the image I saw. I constantly scrutinized myself in the mirror at home and checked my reflection in every car and shop window that I passed. Looking back now and having a better understanding of body image, I realize that my perception of my body was what led me to believe it was too big. The image that I saw impacted my life in a profoundly negative way for many years.

Engaging in self-reflection can significantly improve your comprehension of your perceptual body image. Take a moment to ponder the following questions:

• What do I see when I look in the mirror?
• Am I happy and comfortable with what I see?
• Do I see a body I appreciate and accept?
• Do I see something I don't like and would like to change?
• How many times a day do I feel the need to look in the mirror?
• How much importance do I place on what I see?

Affective Body Image

Affective body image pertains to the emotions evoked based on your feelings about your body. This encompasses how you perceive your body shape, your weight, and specific body parts.

In the past, I experienced strong negative emotions regarding my body, which led to feelings of unhappiness, helplessness, hopelessness and despair. I felt shame, embarrassment and repulsion toward my own reflection. I have put in a lot of work over the years to try and improve my affective body image and can now say that I feel much happier with my body's appearance which in turn results in more positive emotions like contentment and self-confidence when I think of my body.

By reflecting on the following questions, you can gain a deeper and more insightful understanding of your own affective body image:

• How do I feel toward my body?
• Do I have negative or positive feelings about my body?

- Do I feel repulsed by specific parts of my body?
- Do I feel disgusted by my body?
- Do I feel ashamed or embarrassed about my body?
- Do I feel happy and content when I look at my body?
- Do I feel confident when I look at my body?

Cognitive Body Image

Cognitive body image refers to the way in which you think about your body and the beliefs you have about it.

During my childhood, I believed that my body was too big for my age and thought that I would be happier if my body was smaller. This led to obsessive overthinking and a preoccupation with certain parts of my body. My life became consumed by constant thoughts and attempts to change parts of my body, which in turn led to an unhealthy relationship with food and an unhealthy focus on appearance which dominated my life. Today, I think in a completely different way about my body. I believe that my body is strong and healthy and although I am not overjoyed with how some parts of it look, I don't spend time obsessing over wanting to change it.

To gain a deeper understanding of your own cognitive body image, ask yourself these questions:

- What thoughts do I have about my body or specific parts of my body?
- What beliefs do I have about my body?
- Do I spend a lot of time thinking about parts I don't like?
- Do I think about changing my body? If so, how often?
- Do I spend more than an hour a day focusing on this?
- Do I constantly think of my body?
- Do I obsess over my body?
- Does overthinking about my body affect my daily life?
- Do I think my body needs to change to be acceptable?
- What thoughts come up when I think of certain parts of my body? Are they positive or negative?

Behavioural Body Image

Behavioural body image refers to the way in which you behave toward your body. These behaviours may be positive or negative. You might engage in behaviours to change your appearance or disguise your insecurities; or you might be kind to your body by pampering it, feeding it well and engaging in exercise you enjoy.

In the past, I restricted my food intake, engaged in compulsive and punishing exercise routines, and took laxatives in a desperate attempt to lose weight. I would step on scales multiple times a day and would avoid any activity that involved exposing my body. Today I have a more positive behavioural body image. I am a lot kinder to my body. I treat it well by nourishing it daily, I practice yoga and engage in exercise for enjoyment.

Further examples of destructive behaviours that one may engage in include self-induced vomiting, spending money on cosmetic lotions or treatments in an attempt to change one's appearance, covering up in certain clothes or attempting to disguise parts of the body with make-up. Certain individuals may resort to dangerous practices such as extreme dieting, excessive exercise, steroid use, diuretic abuse, diet pill consumption, or even cosmetic surgery.

The following questions can help enhance your self-awareness and bring a clearer understanding of your behavioural body image:

- How do you behave toward your body?
- Do you engage in behaviours to try and change your body or specific parts of your body?
- Are these behaviours healthy, obsessive or dangerous?
- Do you spend a lot of money on treatments or products to try and change your body?
- Would you consider going to extreme lengths like having surgery to change your body?

- Do you wear clothes to try and cover up parts of your body you don't like?
- Are you kind or unkind to your body?

Once you've explored these four facets, hopefully you are better equipped to connect with your own body image and understand its influence on your daily experiences. It is also crucial to recognize that concerns about your body can happen at any age: in childhood, adolescence, as a young adult or in later years. There can be many reasons for people to dislike or obsess over their bodies such as: having too many freckles, feeling too tall or too small, having big ears or teeth that stick out, suffering from hair loss, developing wrinkles or the loss of a youthful body.

The Impact of Body Image

Here are some scenarios that illustrate the impact of body image on an individual.

Scenario 1

A five-year-old boy might stand out as he appears tall for his age. While the child could briefly feel self-conscious if an adult remarks, "You're so much taller than your little friends, aren't you?" and then forget about it within minutes, the same comment could also potentially have a lasting and detrimental impact on his self-esteem and influence the course of his life. It might lead him to constantly question his own adequacy and wish he were shorter.

Had he not been compared to his peers; his height might never have been a source of concern. How a person responds to such comments depends on their individual personality, self-esteem and level of self-confidence. For some such a comment may go over their head; for others it affects the course of their life.

Scenario 2

A man in his thirties might find himself distressed by the onset of hair loss. While a brief pang of sadness and annoyance may cross his mind as he glances in the mirror, he typically carries on with his daily life relatively unaffected. If he veers to the other extreme, he could become intensely self-conscious, spiralling into depression and a sense of helplessness. Overwhelmed by embarrassment and the fear of judgment, he might feel compelled to hide his hair loss with a hat. This emotional struggle could motivate him to seek solutions, including exploring the option of a hair transplant to address his concerns.

Scenario 3

A woman in her sixties might feel a tinge of sadness as she observes the gradual loss of her youthful appearance and reminisces while viewing old photographs. Nonetheless, she typically carries on with her life, acknowledging the inevitable passage of time. Or, she might become consumed by these feelings, spiralling into self-doubt, and developing a strong distaste for her present appearance when contrasted with her younger years. This could lead her to contemplate potential transformations, such as considering Botox injections or even a full surgical facelift to alter her appearance.

These three examples vividly illustrate the profound impact that body image can have on individuals and how it can shape their lives.

Body Image is Always Evolving

When we explore the concept of our body image, it can be valuable to recognize that it is ever changing. It has the capacity to fluctuate not only from one day to the next but even from one moment to the next.

Can you recall a time when you were getting ready for school, college or work, gazed into the mirror and felt confident about your appearance? Yet, on the way there, a sudden glimpse of your reflection in a shop window triggered a wave of self-doubt and discontent with your looks. Your focus abruptly shifted to obsessing over your physical appearance. In this scenario, the reality remains unchanged; your physical body hasn't altered. However, your self-perception has triggered a cascade of negative thoughts and anxiety stemming from your perceived appearance.

I vividly recall experiencing these feelings in the past. I would find myself compulsively scrutinizing my appearance before leaving home, and even though I initially felt satisfied with how I looked, it wouldn't be long before I fixated on a specific aspect of my body. This shift in my mindset was the result of various factors such as a chance glimpse of my reflection in a shop or car window, the clothes I was wearing, or the company I was in or about to meet. Simple things like my dietary choices or whether I had exercised that day could serve as triggers, as well as overhearing conversations about dieting or people's bodies, or receiving comments about my own appearance. Sometimes, no reason or trigger was necessary for a destructive thought pattern to emerge. It is worth remembering that at any given moment, numerous factors can influence how you perceive, feel about, think about, and behave in relation to your body.

Allow me to illustrate this with a specific childhood memory from when I was approximately 10 or 11 years old. On that day, I was a bridesmaid, and in the morning as we set off for the ceremony, I felt relatively content with my appearance. However, as the day progressed and I encountered more people who commented on my dress and my appearance, my self-perception began to change. The more comments I received, I started to feel increasingly self-conscious.

By the end of the day, I had developed an overwhelming sensation of being enormous, and I desperately wanted to hide away to escape these overpowering emotions. The reality was that my body had not undergone any physical changes; it remained the same size as it was in the morning.

This story highlights how our thoughts, feelings and actions about our bodies can strongly influence whether we feel positively or negatively at any given moment about them.

What Does It Mean to Have a Positive Body Image?

It's common to think that having a positive body image means loving every aspect of your body all the time, however, that's not necessarily the case. True body positivity is about embracing your whole self. You may not be thrilled about every part of your body, but you appreciate your natural shape and recognize that physical appearance is just a small part of your identity. You take pride in your body, and while you acknowledge imperfections, you don't dwell on them or obsess over things like your diet, weight or exercise.

Positive body image is about valuing and caring for your body, regardless of your satisfaction with its appearance. It's feeling comfortable and confident in your skin, and appreciating your body's abilities. Positive body image means understanding that your appearance doesn't define your worth or your accomplishments. Your self-esteem is not tied to your looks and your physical appearance doesn't significantly impact your daily life.

Research indicates that feeling good about your body has a positive impact on your mental health and overall wellbeing. Those with a positive body image tend to have more self-compassion, think more positively, and generally experience greater contentment with themselves and their lives. For this exact reason it is important that we try our best to guide our children on the path to develop a positive body image.

Understanding Negative Body Image

People grappling with a negative body image may struggle to accept their appearance, often experiencing shame and discomfort in their own skin. Their self-perception in the mirror may be distorted, leading to obsessive fixation on their perceived flaws, and their self-worth may become overly reliant on appearance. Suffering from a negative body image can trigger a cascade of adverse emotions, affecting various aspects of an individual's life. Consequences may include low self-esteem, feelings of shame, guilt and anxiety, social withdrawal, unhealthy eating patterns, appearance-related obsessions, challenges in relationships, academic or work performance decline, heightened risk of mental health issues like depression or anxiety, and engagement in harmful behaviours such as substance abuse or self-harm.

Speaking from personal experience, I've intimately witnessed the toll that negative body image can have on one's overall wellbeing. There was a time in my life when I'd devote an entire day to obsessing over my body, wrestling with feelings of shame, insecurity, judgment, self-consciousness and a constant sense of feeling that my body was being observed. I felt out of place and anxious in my own skin. My days were consumed by overthinking my food choices, weight and body shape, endlessly searching for ways to transform myself. Every glance in the mirror was an opportunity to berate myself. I was convinced that happiness hinged solely on altering my physical appearance. My self-worth was non-existent. This detrimental way of being took a toll on my relationships, social life, and eventually led to struggles with depression, anxiety and an eating disorder.

As a leading charity for young girls and women, Girlguiding UK's survey 'An Inquiry into Body Image' provides a snapshot of the views of over 2,000 girls and young women, within and outside Girlguiding.

"In 2016, girls and young women aged 11–21 said low body confidence impacted what they felt able to do and the choices they have such as:

- wearing what they like (58%)
- having their picture taken (52%)
- taking part in sport or exercise (39%)
- speaking up in class (36%)"[11]

This research shows that having a negative body image can deeply impact a person's mental and emotional wellbeing in a devastating way.

The Media and Body Image

While I don't attribute all the blame to the media for my negative body image, the unattainable societal standards of the "ideal body" depicted in media certainly exacerbated my feelings. The relentless exposure perpetuated an ongoing cycle of discontent and insecurity.

One of my favourite anti-diet writers, Megan Jayne Crabbe sums it up perfectly in her must-read book, *Body Positive Power*.

"If we don't live up to societal standards of beauty, we see ourselves as failures, burdens and disgraces. We don't just hate our outer shells; we hate our whole selves. And it's exhausting."[12]

Many of us are trapped in this cycle, where it has become our "normal" to constantly compare ourselves to actors, popstars, models, or the latest popular celebrity. We subject our bodies to harsh judgments because they don't conform to the idealized body type. The body that many of us aspire to seems almost unattainable, yet that doesn't deter us from dedicating our lives to pursuing it. The beauty, fitness and diet industries exert immense pressure on us to conform to these narrow beauty standards to feel valued. Weight loss is celebrated, thin bodies are glorified, fat phobia is prevalent, and body-loathing is commonplace. Finding a woman who is truly at peace with her body is a rarity. To genuinely like and accept your body is a form of radicalism in our time. Dr Lauren Muhlheim captures this sentiment perfectly:

"In the Western world a negative body image is so commonplace among women that it is called 'normative discontent' it has become normal to be unhappy."[13]

These days the ideal body looks something like this: curvy but in the right places, stomach is toned and flat, legs and arms are thin and toned, absolutely no cellulite, flawless peachy skin, no body hair, perfect teeth, shaped eyebrows, full lips, no wrinkles, one chin, ample boobs – but not too big.

The "Ideal" Throughout the Decades

As someone who came of age in the 1990s, we were constantly exposed to images of iconic figures like Kate Moss and Jodie Kidd, who defined the beauty and fashion ideals of that era. This subjected us to considerable pressure to emulate their appearance, which, for many, entailed extreme measures like severe dietary restrictions.

The well-known statement by Kate Moss remained firmly etched in our memories.

"Nothing tastes as good as skinny feels."

Throughout the 1990s, there was a pervasive trend toward the emaciated look. Dieting was common practice and although there has been a recent shift toward embracing more curvaceous body types, for as far back as I can remember, a thin body has consistently remained the predominant ideal of beauty.

It's intriguing to observe that in the late 18th and 19th centuries, larger body types were highly regarded, and during times of scarcity, a plump and well-nourished appearance signified affluence. As we transitioned into the 20th century, the "Gibson Girl" emerged as the epitome of the ideal body, characterized by height, slenderness and an exaggerated hourglass figure achieved through tightly laced corsets.

By the 1920s, the concept of dieting gained popularity, giving rise to the fashionable "flapper" look, which emphasized a slender and straight silhouette. If a woman had a hint of breasts, they were bound. The 1930s witnessed a resurgence of appreciation for curves, and by the 1950s, voluptuous figures with small waists – exemplified by icons like Marilyn Monroe and Elizabeth Taylor – became the new ideal. Weight-gain tablets were popular during this era to achieve these curvier looks.

However, the 1960s ushered in a radical shift when model Twiggy burst onto the scene, championing a petite and gaunt appearance, which quickly became the most sought-after look.

In 1963, Weight Watchers was founded, and this marked the beginning of an era when women became fixated on reducing every aspect of their bodies. The 1970s witnessed the rise of a slender, muscular, sun-kissed aesthetic exemplified by *Charlie's Angels* characters.

As the 1980s unfolded, leggy supermodels such as Elle McPherson and Linda Evangelista took the fashion world by storm. The 1990s introduced Kate Moss, bringing the "heroin chic" and grunge-inspired look to the forefront, with thin, waif-like models dominating magazine spreads.

By the early 2000s, artists like Christina Aguilera and Britney Spears were showcasing their sculpted, tanned abdomens, marking a shift toward a more toned and athletic ideal.

It's only within the past decade that we've witnessed a resurgence of curvier body types in the media, with the "bootylicious" look gaining prominence, largely due to the influence of figures like the Kardashians, Nicki Minaj and Beyoncé. In 2015, the very first plus-sized model graced the runway, followed by fashion designer Christian Siriano incorporating plus-sized models into his show at New York Fashion Week the following year.

In that same year, a line of Barbie dolls representing diverse body types was introduced, and the reality show *Project Runway* featured plus-sized models for the first time. Is this a definitive shift away from the "thin-is-in" mentality? The answer remains uncertain. However, what's clear is the current trend of enhancing certain body areas with fat injections to align with the current beauty ideal highlights the evolving and sometimes contradictory nature of beauty standards.

In the past decade, there has been a noticeable intensification of body preoccupation, exacerbated by the prevalence of platforms like Instagram and the rise of "selfie culture". The appearance of our bodies is a subject of significant interest and importance to many.

While the ideals of beauty continue to evolve, their unceasing impact on our lives remains constant. In this digital age, there's no escaping the pervasive influence of diet culture. Pop-up advertisements inundate us, consistently emphasizing the pursuit of the so-called "perfect body". For so many, the way our body looks is of huge interest and importance. Although standards of beauty are ever changing, their impact on our lives is constant and understanding the impact of how this affects our body image is crucial.

Reflection Brings About Change

In this chapter, we have delved into the definitions of body image and demonstrated the ever-changing nature of the "ideal" body. Hopefully, you now possess a more comprehensive understanding of your own relationship with body image and how the media's portrayal of the "perfect body" can influence your self-perception.

Gaining deeper insight into how you perceive, feel, think and behave in relation to your own body can help you discern whether your body image is positive, negative, or subject to fluctuations. The concept of body image and its definition may have been unfamiliar territory for you, and it might be the first time you've contemplated the impact of your body image on your daily life. It's possible that you've spent a significant portion of your life thinking and acting in certain ways without fully recognizing the profound effect your body image can have in your life.

In summary, body image is an intricate and multifaceted concept that encompasses our thoughts, emotions and attitudes toward our physical appearance. It wields a profound influence on our mental, emotional and physical wellbeing. A positive body image entails the acceptance and respect of one's body, regardless of its shape or size. Conversely, a negative body image involves feelings of dissatisfaction, shame or embarrassment regarding one's appearance.

The societal beauty ideal, perpetuated by the media, advertising and popular culture, exerts a significant impact on our beliefs and attitudes concerning our bodies. The constant inundation of images and messages promoting a narrow definition of beauty can foster unrealistic expectations, body dissatisfaction and even mental health issues such as eating disorders, anxiety and depression.

Nurturing a positive body image necessitates a focus on self-care, self-compassion, and self-love. This entails learning to appreciate and celebrate one's body for its capabilities rather than fixating solely on its aesthetics. By adopting a more holistic and accepting approach to our bodies, we can lead happier, healthier lives, thereby positively influencing the wellbeing of future generations, including our children.

3

HOW IS BODY IMAGE FORMED?

We all have thousands of experiences throughout our childhood which shape the formation of our beliefs and thoughts we have about our bodies. We absorbed the thin-equals-happy message loud and clear at a young age and the fear of gaining weight was very real. In this chapter we will explore what factors may have contributed to the relationship that you have with your body today. It will trigger you to recall some childhood memories and experiences to make sense of the messages you picked up about your physical self. You will delve into how specific messages influenced the way you think, feel and behave with regards to your body. This will help to give you a clearer understanding of how our children learn, how they pick up messages, and the many ways that contribute to the formation of their body image.

If our collective goal and the aim of this book is to maximize the likelihood of our children developing a positive body image, we must first understand how our own relationship with our body was formed. What we are taught about our bodies as children has a massive impact on how we see ourselves as adults. Looking deeper into where our own perceptions come from and what influenced these beliefs will help us to understand how we can communicate better with children.

Diet Culture is Inescapable

To start, it's essential to keep in mind a fundamental aspect of our society: we are constantly exposed to diet culture and inundated with daily messages that convey the idea that our body size is intricately tied to our value. This influence begins from the moment we come into this world. Indeed, even when a new baby is born, the first question asked is often, "What did he/she weigh?" This preoccupation with weight and body size begins from the day we are born, and the misguided belief that a smaller body equates to a superior and more deserving body has persisted for generations.

Glennon Doyle's words in her book *Untamed* resonate deeply:

> *"Glennon Doyle's words in her book* Untamed *resonate deeply, "we become the air we breathe"*[14]

We swim in it from the day we enter the world.

As children, we are inundated with a multitude of messages that we gradually internalize. The influence of media messaging looms large in shaping our perceptions of body image, bombarding us with countless depictions of unrealistic "ideal" bodies via movies, television, magazines and advertisements. The fashion and beauty industries exert considerable influence, dictating how bodies should conform to a certain standard, and was constantly thrust upon us during our upbringing. Even the toys we played with carried messages about body ideals, and the opinions and attitudes of our peers regarding appearance undoubtedly left their mark.

The activities and interests pursued during childhood will have significantly influenced your perception of your body, particularly if there was an emphasis on body size and conforming to certain appearance standards. The perspectives and comments of influential figures in your life, such as parents, caregivers, other family members, teachers, doctors and nurses, undoubtedly contributed to your beliefs about weight, shape, body size, dietary choices and calorie consumption. As a child, you may have unconsciously absorbed implicit messages and behaviours demonstrated by these authority figures. Experiences like being teased or placed on restrictive diets may have had a profound impact. Furthermore, your personality traits, genetic makeup, and the presence of disabilities or disfigurements may have also played a role in shaping your body image. As you can see, numerous factors have collectively shaped your feelings and attitudes toward your body.

Reflection
Before delving into some of the factors that influence our body image, take a moment to consider or make note of responses to the following questions.

- Can you remember when you first became aware of your body?
- Did you feel too tall, too small, too fat, too thin, too big?
- Did people ever comment on your size?
- Were you made fun of by elders, siblings or at school because of your body?
- Did you feel confident in your sports kit?
- What toys did you play with?
- What movies and programmes did you enjoy?
- What pop stars and actors did you admire?
- What magazines did you buy or were you exposed to?
- What were your friend's attitudes toward appearance?
- What sports or hobbies did you enjoy?
- Did you ever feel that you should diet or wish you could change parts of your body?
- What was the attitude toward food in your house?
- Did people comment on your food intake or tease you about it?
- Were you aware of bathroom scales, calories and diets as a child?

- Were you ever put on a diet?
- Were you taught to be proud of your body and appreciate its function?
- What personality traits did you have?
- Did you have any disabilities as a child?
- Do you remember how your parents/caregivers spoke about food, weight and bodies?
- Did your role models diet and have a desire to be smaller?
- Were you privy to conversations about diets, weight loss, body shaming, body worshipping?
- Did your elders have respect for their own bodies?
- Did they berate themselves in front of you?
- Did they compare themselves to others?
- Did your elders glorify thin and demonize fat?
- Did your body ever hold you back from doing something (attending an event, going swimming, dating)?
- Did the way you look ever make you feel unworthy?
- Did the way you feel about your body ever affect your mental health?
- Have you ever resorted to extreme or dangerous methods to try and lose weight?

The Roots of My Body Image

Contemplating my own life and considering the questions posed in the box, it becomes evident that various factors shaped the development of my body image. These include my personality traits, the influence of my peers, the toys I played with, the magazines I encountered, the celebrities I admired, the activities I participated in, and most notably, the messages I absorbed from the adults in my life. The deeply ingrained beliefs I formed about my body primarily stemmed from my home environment, where I observed, listened and emulated behaviours and attitudes.

From an early age, I was immersed in conversations about diets and body shapes and sizes. I witnessed every adult in my life relentlessly attempting to reduce their body size through dieting, calorie counting, an obsession with food and the number on the scale. I listened attentively as my elders celebrated weight loss in themselves and others, instilling in me a deep-seated dread of gaining weight, which I internalized as a fear.

As a young child, I vividly recall my daily battles with my body and the compulsive relationship I had with my reflection. I scrutinized myself relentlessly, repeatedly checking and rechecking, desperately searching for an angle that would make me appear thinner, all in the pursuit of fleeting happiness. This led to a pattern of restricting my food intake and excessive exercise – daily weigh-ins became my norm. Any minor weight loss only intensified the constant pressure to maintain or lose even more, never reaching a point of satisfaction. These daily self-criticisms and preoccupations with food and weight quickly evolved into obsessions. The messages I absorbed about my body during my childhood had a profoundly detrimental impact on my school years and early adulthood, casting a dark shadow over my life.

The Birth of Body Image

As discussed in chapter one we are born with absolutely no judgments at all toward our physical selves. We are not born hating our bodies. As a baby we don't wish to weigh less or have thinner thighs. We don't think our bodies are too fat or too thin, or believe our nose is too big or our hair too curly. Up to a certain age "chubby" is considered cute – I'm not sure at what point that view of a child's body changes and becomes something to be ashamed of. All the messages we receive about our bodies are learned.

From a very early age, children begin to develop an awareness of their bodies. As toddlers they start recognizing themselves in the mirror. By preschool age, they begin comparing their bodies to those of their friends and absorbing the behaviours and attitudes of adults regarding food, body shapes and weight. Participating in activities like dance, cheerleading and gymnastics exposes them to messages about appearance and size. The way teachers, nurses and doctors communicate also leaves an impression, often with long-lasting effects.

As children progress through school, the opinions of their peers regarding appearance start to influence them. When puberty arrives, things become more complex. Adolescents become more attuned to body size, physical changes, comments from others, clothing choices and develop an intensified focus on appearance. Self-esteem can fluctuate during this period, leading many to believe that being thinner is the solution to fitting in – after all, it has been ingrained since birth that thinner means happier, more successful, more attractive. It is at this stage that many become victims to diet culture, and begin clinging to a coping mechanism that promises a better life. Who could blame them?

It's important to recognize that having concerns about one's body and appearance is a common experience, particularly during adolescence. While it's natural to think about these aspects, it's crucial not to let them become obsessive or hinder one's ability to enjoy life.

Let's take a closer look at our own experiences and try to drill down into the primary factors that have shaped our current perceptions of our bodies.

Media Messaging and Body Image

Throughout our childhoods we were exposed to thousands of unrealistic images of bodies and were bombarded by diet culture messaging every day, most of the time without noticing or realizing it. These messages were internalized through our subconscious.

In the eighties I remember we shopped from catalogues and there was never a model used who was more than a size 10. If you are old enough, can you recall ever seeing a fat model in a magazine, on a billboard, in a catalogue or an advert, or a mannequin in a shop window that wasn't slim? I recall looking at these images of women and thinking how perfect they looked with a dream that one day I would look like that. Societal beauty ideals and messaging from the fashion and beauty industry were hard to escape.

When you recall the movies and programmes you enjoyed, it is likely that the main characters were always thin and beautiful with perfect skin. As children we most likely drooled over photos of our favourite Disney princess characters, unaware that these bodies were not even real. The pop stars and actors we admired and dreamed of looking like were always one body type. Sandy from *Grease* was the first one that stood out for me.

What we saw everywhere were bodies that were very thin and toned and certainly had no blemishes, lumps, bumps, back fat or tummy rolls. Most magazines you would have been exposed to were covered in photographs of perfectly proportioned models, actors and pop stars with details of their diet and exercise regime along with a promise that you could one day look like that if you followed their daily routine.

Do you remember diet adverts on TV promising you the perfect "beach body" and the adverts in your local community centre, school and doctor's surgery with huge banners advertising slimming clubs? Everywhere we looked as kids the media sent us a message that we had to get thinner.

Reflection
Ask yourself the following questions to gain a deeper understanding of how the media might have impacted your body image as you were growing up.

- What images do you remember being exposed to?
- Do you remember what movies, programmes, cartoons you enjoyed as a child?

- What societal ideal was portrayed in the media at the time of you growing up?
- Did you dream of looking like those you admired?
- Did you compare your body to your favourite actors and popstars?
- Looking back, what do you think the media taught you about your body while growing up?
- Did you ever feel pressured to look a certain way?
- Did you ever start methods to try and change the shape of your body because of an image you were exposed to?

Toys and Body Image

Many of the toys we played with during our childhood presented us with an idealized and unrealistic portrayal of body shapes from a very early age. The measurements and forms of perfectly sculpted bodies, such as those of Barbie dolls, Disney princesses and superheroes have been – and continue to be – far from a reflection of reality. It's not limited to girls: consider Barbie's boyfriend with his muscular and impeccably defined physique or the Hulk with his bulging biceps. As children, we perceive these figures as genuine and flawless, often aspiring to imitate them and yearning to look like them in our dreams.

I have a vivid memory of comparing the size of my legs and waist to those of my Barbie dolls and feeling somewhat disheartened, even as a very young child, because I understood that it would be unattainable for me to ever match these proportions. I also recall asking for a 'Girls World' with dark hair and my mum informing me that Santa couldn't find one. What kind of message did that convey? Body diversity wasn't a concept in those times. It's only recently that we've started to see more diverse dolls become available on the market.

Reflection

Consider how the toys you played with as a kid might have impacted your body image as you were growing up.

- Do you remember the toys you played with as a child?
- Do you remember comparing your body to your Barbies or Disney princesses?
- Do you feel that this influenced the way you felt about your own body?

Peers and Body Image

Peers wield considerable influence over an individual's body image, as the social sphere becomes a mirror reflecting perceived standards and ideals. If our friends place emphasis on appearance and body size, it may have had a significant influence on our own body image development. You may have grown up with friends who made comments about your size or even teased you about it. If at some point dieting was the "in" chat, you may have been compelled to take part to feel part of the crowd.

Comparisons with peer appearances and societal beauty norms can trigger self-consciousness, fostering a desire to conform. Constructive or destructive comments from peers can significantly impact self-esteem, either nurturing a positive self-image or cultivating insecurities. The quest for acceptance within a peer group may drive individuals to adopt certain appearance-related behaviours – from dieting to emulation of fashion trends – further entrenching the influence of peers on shaping perceptions of one's own body. The impact of peer interactions on body image is profound and multifaceted.

I personally always felt larger compared to my friends and believed that I should strive to become smaller like them. Being aware of wearing a larger dress size than most of my peers made me feel extremely self-conscious and ashamed.

Reflection

Consider the following questions to better understand how your peers may have influenced how you feel about your body.

- Do you believe your peers played a role in shaping your body image?
- Do you remember if there was a focus on size or appearance amongst your friends?
- Were you teased because of your size?
- Were you aware of the size of your clothes compared to your friends?
- Did you compare your body size to that of your friends?

Personality Traits

Individuals with a perfectionist, high-achieving personality tend to be more self-critical and can be particularly sensitive or susceptible to external influences. While a comment about body size may not significantly affect one child, it can deeply impact another and linger with them throughout their life.

I can personally relate to this; I was quite demanding of myself, always striving to excel, and had a rigid mindset that required me to be the best at everything I undertook. If I didn't give 100 percent effort, I felt like a failure. These feelings eventually projected onto how I felt about my body.

Reflection

Reflecting on these following questions may help you understand if your personality traits contributed to how your body image formed.

- Were you hard on yourself as a kid?
- Were you a high achiever at school?

- Were you a perfectionist?
- Were you a people-pleaser?
- Do you feel that your any specific personality traits contributed to the way you feel about your body?

Childhood Activities

The activities you participated in during your childhood might have left you more susceptible to body dissatisfaction. Body size and shape often become focal points in clubs such as dancing, ballet, boxing, cheerleading, gymnastics, athletics, football and boxing clubs.

I can recall being part of an athletics club and feeling self-conscious about being larger than my peers, constantly comparing myself to them.

Your body size may not have been a concern or even on your radar until it was brought to your attention. I vividly remember reading the late Nikki Graham's book about her lifelong battle with an eating disorder, which tragically claimed her life. In her account, she attributed the beginning of her struggles to a gymnastics teacher who made a comment about the size of her bum.

Reflection
Consider whether you think the clubs or activities you enjoyed as a child played a role in shaping your feelings about your body.

- What clubs did you attend as a child?
- Was your size or shape pointed out to you?
- Were you told you were too big or too small?
- Were you advised to diet or lose weight?

Teasing and Body Image

Teasing or receiving comments about one's body can instil a belief that something is inherently "wrong" with your appearance and can significantly impact body image. Whether the teasing pertains to being too small, too big, or having a distinctive feature like a large nose, the effects can endure long into adulthood.

It's important to note that teasing can be influential, regardless of whether it comes from an adult or a peer, and it can lead a child to believe there's something fundamentally flawed about them. This, in turn, may prompt them to engage in harmful behaviours to alter their body and avoid such unwanted attention.

I distinctly recall being teased about my body size, and at the time, it felt like the world was ending. It had a profoundly negative effect on my life and led me down a path of strict dieting and punishing exercise routines.

Reflection

Reflect on whether you think being teased about your body size had an impact on your body image.

- Were you made fun of because of your appearance by elders, by peers or siblings?
- Did people use derogatory names or make insults related to your body?

Adults' Conversations and Behaviour

In our early years, family and close contacts play a pivotal role in shaping our body image. As a child, you were likely exposed to numerous conversations where adults made remarks concerning body shapes and weight, and you absorbed these messages both consciously and subconsciously. If you regularly witnessed a parent expressing dissatisfaction with their appearance, passing judgment on others based on their looks, or making a significant issue out of food, it could influence how much importance you attach to physical appearance.

Hearing our elders refer to themselves as ugly or fat, and constantly striving to lose weight, can lead us to grow up with the belief that being thin is the only acceptable way to be, instilling a fear of anything other than a thin body. Children internalize the messages they hear. We can't underestimate the power of subconscious programming in our children.

In my personal experience, this was particularly noticeable. I actively observed my elders ridiculing and gossiping about bodies they considered less than "perfect". I witnessed their persistent efforts to reduce their own body size. Their deep admiration for petite, slender physiques left a lasting impression on me, significantly emphasizing the importance of being in a thin body.

Reflection

Were you exposed to discussions about diets, weights, and body sizes during your upbringing? Did you overhear or were you privy to any of the following types of comments?

- "She's lucky – such a petite little thing."
- "He is so small for his age."
- "I wish I never ate that; I'll pay for it!"
- "She is so huge now; she has really let herself go recently!"
- "How much did you lose?"
- "What diet are you on?"
- "Those jeans are so slimming!"
- "Have you lost weight? You look great – share your secrets."
- "Argh, the diet is ruined! I will start again on Monday."
- "I'll burn it off at the gym."

If you heard similar comments growing up or were exposed to such conversations about body size, do you believe they had an impact on your body image?

Direct Comments About Body Image

Remarks directly targeted at children regarding their body size or eating habits can profoundly shape the development of their body image. If you were exposed to comments about your appearance or your food intake as a child, it possibly drew attention to something you were possibly not aware of previously.

I clearly recall my elders making comments about my food consumption and my size and, although their intentions were never malicious, they had a profoundly negative effect on the development of my relationship with food and my body.

Can you recall hearing comments like this while growing up?

- "I can't believe how big you are now."
- "You'll need to watch ..."
- "You won't always get away with eating so much."
- "You got that nose from your ..."
- "Look how many freckles you have!"
- "You are so huge/small compared to ..."
- "You're tiny, you will never need to worry."
- "Where do you put it?"
- "You are a right pie muncher, aren't you?"
- "Have you not had enough?"
- "Wow! Someone was hungry."
- "Are you really going to eat all that?"
- "I could never eat all that!"

Reflection
It might be beneficial to dedicate some time to reflect and revisit the memories of what you heard as a child.

- Were there any significant moments that stand out?
- Was your size pointed out to you?
- Did your elders comment on your weight?

- Do you remember what you heard as a child with regards to food, weight and body size?
- What did you notice about the behaviours of your elders when it came to food, weight and bodies?
- Were you privy to conversations about diets and weight loss?

Genetics and Body Image

The role of genetics in shaping our body image is an intricate and often-overlooked aspect of our self-perception. Genetics contributes to the physical traits we inherit from our parents, which include our body shape, size, and even how we metabolize food. These genetic predispositions can influence how we perceive ourselves and how others perceive us. For instance, if we inherit a body type that tends to be naturally thin, we may feel more positively about our body image. Conversely, if our genetics lean toward a different body shape, we might struggle with body image issues, especially in a society that idealizes a specific body standard. Moreover, genetics can impact our susceptibility to weight gain or difficulty in losing weight, which can further affect our body image and self-esteem. You could eat the same as the next person and exercise the same and you would still be a completely different shape and size.

When I reflected on my experiences with genetics, I realized that no matter how much I attempted to starve myself in the nineties I was never ever going to be the size or shape of Kate Moss. Even as a kid I realized that the likelihood of ever having the same measurements as my Barbie dolls was way out of my reach. Understanding the genetic component of our body image can help us appreciate the unique and diverse range of body types and foster a healthier relationship with our own.

Reflection

- Do you believe that your genetic make-up contributed to your body image?
- Were you aware that because of your genetic predisposition a certain body type may be unattainable?

Disability and Body Image

Having a disability or disfigurement can significantly impact an individual's development of body image. Society often perpetuates narrow standards of beauty, which can lead to feelings of inadequacy or self-consciousness for those who deviate from these norms. Individuals with disabilities or disfigurements may experience social stigma, discrimination, or the internalization of negative societal perceptions, influencing their self-esteem and body image. Coping with physical challenges may contribute to a complex relationship with one's body.

Reflection

If you have a disability or a disfigurement, how do you feel that it affected the development of your body image?

- Do you feel that your life was more difficult?
- Was the disability/disfigurement difficult to accept?
- Did you dream of not having the disability/disfigurement?

Knowledge Is Power

After exploring all the aspects of what influences body image, you maybe now understand better your relationship with your body. As children we see, we hear, and we copy. We are gullible and vulnerable and receptive. The thousands of messages we picked up throughout our childhood massively influences our body image.

If our aim is to prioritize healthy role modelling to help children develop a positive body image there are many things we can do to help them. The knowledge on this topic begins with us at home. We have a lot of power over our children, and we have the tools to shape them to think differently about their bodies and food.

In conclusion, the development of our body image is a multifaceted journey, influenced by an intricate interplay of factors including diet culture messaging, the impact of social media, childhood toys, childhood activities, the opinions of peers, societal ideals, the lasting effects of teasing, direct comments from adults, subtle subliminal messaging, and even the genetic blueprint we inherit. By delving into this complex web of influences, we gain valuable insights into our own body image and, more importantly, how children navigate this terrain today.

Understanding the origins of our own body image allows us to empathize with the challenges children face in their formative years. Armed with this knowledge, we are better equipped to guide and support the next generation in their journey toward developing a positive body image. By fostering an environment that values individuality, diversity and self-acceptance, we can empower children to grow up with a strong sense of self-worth, resilience and a profound appreciation for the uniqueness of their bodies.

In the chapters that follow, we will explore strategies and practical steps to help children navigate the ever-evolving landscape of body image, empowering them to emerge with confidence, self-love and a positive outlook on their bodies. Ultimately, by sharing our insights and experiences, we can collectively work toward a world where every child grows up feeling positive about their body, ready to face life's challenges with resilience and a sense of self-worth that knows no bounds.

4

THROUGH THE EYES OF A CHILD

Imagine being a child again, wide-eyed and impressionable, taking in the world around you with an innocent curiosity. You are not yet burdened with the weight of societal expectations, body standards or the complexities of adult life. Your world is filled with wonder, and every moment is a new opportunity to learn and grow.

But amid this innocence, there is a powerful force at play – a force that shapes your perceptions, moulds your beliefs and leaves an indelible mark on your self-image. That force is the influence of the adults in your life – their words, their actions, and their attitudes toward weight, bodies and food.

As a child, you absorb the messages they unwittingly send, often without question. You listen intently to their conversations, you watch how they treat their own bodies, and you learn to interpret their comments about yours. These early experiences lay the foundation for your lifelong relationship with your body and food.

In this chapter, we step into the shoes of that impressionable child and explore the world as they see it. We listen through their ears, we observe through their eyes, and we feel through their hearts. We examine the messages they receive from the adults in their lives – messages that can either uplift and empower or wound and scar.

Through personal testimonies, we hear from individuals who, as children, absorbed the comments, judgments and attitudes of the adults around them. We gain insight into how these messages affected their self-esteem, body image and overall wellbeing. Their stories remind us of the profound impact our words and actions may have on the next generation.

How Our Role Models Shape Us

As children enter this world, they hold no judgments about their bodies. However, as time goes on, they are taught that their bodies are flawed, that they are something that needs constant fixing, altering and manipulation. Children naturally admire and learn from the adult role models in their lives. When these adults display an obsession with losing weight, body sizes, diets and food it becomes a huge challenge to expect their children to develop the opposite – a positive relationship with food and their bodies.

As we enter the world of a child, where innocence and vulnerability intersect with the complexities of adult influence, we will explore the power of words, the weight of societal expectations, and the opportunity we all have to nurture a healthier, more positive environment for our children to grow, thrive, and embrace their bodies with love and acceptance.

My upbringing revolved around a family culture that celebrated weight loss and normalized fat shaming. Family members placed immense importance on topics such as food, diets, body weights and sizes. My early beliefs about my body, food and weight were undoubtedly influenced by overhearing adult conversations, absorbing the connotations of comments made about people's body sizes, dietary choices, and the significance of the number on a scale. Thin bodies were idealized, praised – almost revered, while fat bodies were subject to shame and ridicule. The scale's reading and clothing sizes held tremendous significance, and calorie counting was a routine part of daily life. "Being good" meant adhering to a diet of predominantly low-fat foods, while "being bad" was breaking that diet by indulging in a "forbidden" or "fattening" treat. Throughout my childhood, I frequently witnessed the overwhelming despair, sadness and disappointment expressed by my elders during weigh-in nights at the local slimming club when their progress didn't meet their expectations, or when they felt "too fat" or strayed from their diets.

Exposure to such a multitude of comments undeniably contributed to my development of a negative body image and planted a seed that led to the development of an eating disorder.

Words Hold Power

The subsequent remarks concerning food, weight and body image are frequently uttered in the presence of children. I have included examples that were familiar to me during my own childhood, as well as some which are commonly heard today.

While you read the comments, attempt to empathize from a child's perspective and to approach each comment with a sense of genuine curiosity.

Mum has some cake and remarks: **"I wish I never ate that; I'll pay for it."**

A child may perceive that their mother has engaged in a negative behaviour and conclude that abstaining from cake is necessary to avoid feelings of guilt. The child might express a desire for their mother to refrain from consuming cake in the future, as they genuinely don't want her to experience any negative emotions. It could lead them to adopt the belief that eating cake is inherently "bad" if it elicits such reactions in their mother. Consequently, their own food choices may be influenced, as they avoid similar items to prevent encountering similar negative emotions.

A child overhears an adult conversation: **"Did you see the size of her? She has really let herself go!"**

In the child's perception, they come to understand that this person's physical appearance has changed and pick up that, because the person has put on weight, this change is negative. They become aware that the adult discusses other people's bodies and notices changes in their own body size. They pick up that body size carries significance. Additionally, they may sense the negative implications of these discussions and fear being spoken about in such a manner. A child's thoughts may revolve around the idea of staying small, fearing the possibility of being subjected to similar comments if they were to gain weight.

If the child is already overweight, they may internalize the belief that being fat or putting on weight is a negative thing and take steps to become smaller. What becomes evident to them is the profound aversion to having their body scrutinized and experiencing disappointment or judgment from others. The child begins to perceive the importance of being thin.

After stepping on the scales, an elated mum runs through and declares to the family: **"I've lost four pounds ... brilliant! I need to be good the rest of the week."**

A child perceives their mother's happiness and begins to associate losing weight as a positive thing. They may be confused and wonder how their mother will manage to "be good". They might contemplate the idea that eating less and adhering to diet plans could be the key to achieving such happiness. Additionally, they may develop an awareness of bathroom scales and view the number that they display as a determinant of happiness. They learn that this number holds significance in their mother's life. Consequently, they understand that scales are important and that the information they reveal can evoke feelings of joy or sadness. They may be tempted to jump on the scale to check the number.

On hearing the following statement followed by laughter: **"Look at daddy's fat tummy – it's so funny!"**

Based on a casual remark, a child may infer that to have a "fat tummy" brings ridicule, implying that it is unacceptable to possess anything other than a flat or toned tummy. They may internalize the belief that they should avoid having a fat tummy at all costs for fear of being mocked. While such a comment may initially appear light-hearted, it has the potential to plant a seed in the child's mind, instilling a strong desire to never be fat due to the possibility of becoming a target of laughter and ridicule.

A statement such as: **"She is lovely and slim – she must be a size 8. She is so lucky."**

Upon hearing such a remark, a child may grasp the notion that being considered attractive or lovely is contingent upon being slim. The emphasis placed on body size underscores its significance, with a UK size 8 (US size 10) being perceived as desirable. They may internalize the importance assigned to having a slender physique. Furthermore, they learn that it is socially acceptable and commonplace to make comments about other people's bodies. Consequently, they may self-impose pressure to conform to a specific appearance, as they recognize it as a crucial aspect of societal importance.

Cake is on the table and mum says: **"I better not eat that; I need to be good."**

The child may form the belief that if their mother eats this specific food, they are bad. They might experience confusion and curiosity, wondering why their mother is restricted from eating it. As a result, they may adopt a similar restriction and eliminate that food from their own diet.

Mum is getting ready for a party and her clothes don't fit. On hearing: **"I really wish I could just fit into that dress. I look horrible."**

The child immediately becomes aware of the unhappiness experienced by their mother and picks up on the desperation in her voice. They may feel sad because they don't like witnessing their mum feeling unhappy. This reinforces in the child's mind the significance of body size and the perceived necessity of becoming smaller. The child's empathy for their mother's emotional distress further reinforces the idea that achieving a smaller size is linked to happiness.

Another example: **"You should see the amount of weight she has put on – she is huge now."**

When a child overhears such a comment, they internalize the idea that gaining weight is exceptionally negative. The concept of weight gain becomes an undesirable prospect in their life, something they actively seek to avoid. Consequently, their weight assumes importance and begins to exert pressure on them to maintain a small body.

There are hundreds of comments our children are exposed to that are laden with diet culture. Here are a few more for you to ponder.

- "A minute on the lips, a lifetime on the hips."
- "Those jeans are so slimming."
- "You've lost so much weight, you look great. What's your secret?"
- "I need to be good."
- "I'm wearing this to cover up the sins."
- "She's put the beef on!"
- "Look at the figure on her!"
- "Today is a cheat day – I'll hit the gym tomorrow."

Such comments have been a recurring presence throughout my life, consistently conveying the same underlying message:

- Losing weight is good.
- Gaining weight is bad.

- To look good your body must be small.
- Scales are important and a measure of worth.
- Body size is important.
- It is okay to comment on other people's size.
- It's okay to laugh at fat bodies.
- Some foods are bad.
- It's normal to diet.
- Bodies are scrutinized and judged due to their size.

It's important to recognize that the previously mentioned comments aren't likely to be said *directly* to children but are nonetheless subconsciously absorbed, exerting a profound influence on a child's perception of food and their body.

Direct Comments

Now let's consider the impact of comments made directly to a child.

Whether they are positive or negative, accidental or well-intended, words hold the power to exert a significant influence on a child's self-esteem and body image, often resulting in awful consequences. Negative remarks can induce feelings of shame and embarrassment about their physicality, fostering low self-worth and the potential development of body image concerns. On the other hand, well-intentioned positive comments may inadvertently convey the idea that a child's value is contingent upon their appearance, thereby encouraging an unhealthy preoccupation with their body while downplaying other vital facets of their identity.

Many of us inadvertently make comments about a child's size, often well-intentioned or as part of a greeting or conversation filler. Yet we often underestimate the potential impact of such remarks. While some children may not be significantly affected by a comment about their body, for others, a single comment has the potential to sow the seeds of lifelong insecurities.

The following examples illustrate some casual remarks frequently made by adults to children:

- "You've gotten so big!"
- "I can't believe how huge you are!"
- "Look at the size of you now!"
- "You can eat!"
- "Where do you put it all?!"
- "You are like a bottomless pit!"
- "You like your grub!"
- "Have you got hollow legs?"
- "How did you manage to eat all that?!"
- "You are a big eater!"
- "Look at the size of you, so petite."
- "Look at those chubby cheeks!"
- "You're a very big girl for your age, aren't you?"
- "You've put weight on – don't worry, it's just puppy fat."
- "You are HUGE compared to ... and you are the same age!"
- "Aww you are so tiny. You are lucky."
- "You will never need to worry."
- "You won't always be this tiny – watch out!"

Drawing attention to these types of comments is not to cast blame or shame on the adults who make them. The primary aim for including them is to raise awareness. The intention is to underscore the potential harm seemingly flippant comments may cause and to emphasize their enduring influence. It's a common social practice to remark on a child's size when we haven't seen them in a while, and many of us have, at some point, been guilty of doing so. These comments often slip out unconsciously, as they seem almost instinctive.

When we comment on a child's size, our intention may be to offer a compliment by acknowledging their growth or changes in stature. However, it's important to consider that we might be bringing attention to something the child had not previously been conscious of, which could potentially make them feel self-conscious or uneasy. We must bear in mind that while some children may not fully comprehend or take offense at remarks about their appearance, others may be more sensitive to such comments and could be adversely affected by them. So, it is crucial for us to exercise mindfulness regarding the potential impact of our words on children.

Nikki Grahame, author of *Fragile* who tragically passed away in 2021 after suffering a gruelling battle with anorexia since early childhood, said she clearly remembers one comment when getting changed for gymnastics: "Haven't you got a big bum, Nikki?". She remembers feeling embarrassed and going home to analyse her bum. She quotes: "I guess that's how it all began."[15]

Sharing Childhood Experiences

Throughout the years, I've heard countless stories from individuals who've recounted how a single comment about their weight or body size during their childhood heightened their awareness of it, resulting in the formation of a lasting complex that continues to impact them well into adulthood. A seemingly innocuous and offhand remark, akin to the examples mentioned earlier, can harbour much more harm than we might comprehend. It possesses the potential to significantly erode the confidence of a sensitive child or lay the groundwork for the development of an eating disorder.

I have been fortunate enough to collaborate with individuals who have graciously opened up about the comments they received regarding their size or eating habits. Their brave accounts shed light on how such remarks served as catalysts for lifelong battles with body image, food-related challenges, and the onset of eating disorders. Their names have been changed to protect their identity.

Marianne, 50, has experience of bulimia and binge eating since she was 18. She clearly remembers a school nurse saying,

"Remember to tell your mum about your pot belly" – she was just 5 years old and vividly recalls standing there in her navy-blue gym knickers feeling humiliated and ashamed of her body. When she was eight, she remembers being on holiday and her brother saying he was embarrassed to be with her because she was so fat. He also used to tease her. At aged 12 her mum told her she was too fat for a specific style of school skirt. It was at this age that she went on her first diet using a food substitute called "prefill" which was bought for her by her mum. This triggered an obsession with dieting and desperately wanting to lose weight. Aged 14 she says she started using food to cheer herself up. At 18 she started to make herself throw up. She says she never felt good enough and felt she didn't fit in. She feels that the comments led her to constantly compare herself to others, something she that she still does. She says: "I was so self-conscious of my body – still am! I think I wanted my mum to feel proud of me and I never seemed to get this validation." She has never had professional help for her eating disorder.

Rena, 54, has experience of anorexia and bulimia. When she was 13 her mother gave her two pairs of control pants as a Christmas present. Rena says: "I remember to this day the shame of receiving these, the suggestion was that I was too fat! At that point I think that the seed was planted that I really could not be allowed to gain any more weight, that I had to lose it instead." Aged 14 she vividly remembers losing weight after a bad dose of flu – "I looked ghastly, very pale and was lethargic, but of course a loss in weight was seen as a huge bonus." Her weight loss was complemented, and she was congratulated for it. She feels that this was a definite trigger for the start of her lifetime struggle with anorexia. Rena strongly believes in the importance of congratulating children on their achievements and not on what they look like. She also feels that the mention of calories in front of children should be forbidden; there was a lot of emphasis on this when she was growing up. She has recently spent three months in hospital as her daily battle with her eating disorder continues.

Janine, 36, has struggled with her body image since she was a child. She started dieting aged only 10. She said her parents always made her feel that she was too big. Her dad often used to say to her, "I don't know where you come from – you're so big, big boned!" She said: "I felt like there was something wrong with me and the best thing to be was little like them." If she lost weight her parents would complement her and say, "Oh, that's better" or, "Hasn't she done well?" Janine says this continued all the way through childhood and adolescence. She said: "I always wanted the recognition from my dad, based on how slim I was." She started going to slimming clubs with her mum aged 14 and got praised when she stuck to her diet. She often heard her mum say, "Oh I haven't had anything to eat today" and says she could sense how proud she was because she could survive on such little food. Her mum also used to comment if people lost weight, with, "Oh doesn't she look good, she's lost so much weight!". If someone had put on weight she would say, "What a shame", like it was something awful, something really terrible. Janine said she still compares herself to others, still searches for the perfect diet to try and make herself smaller. She recognizes that she binges on food to help her deal with her emotions. She has never sought help.

Joy, 27, has suffered from anorexia and bulimia in the past. She says that although the comments she heard about food and weight were not the cause of her of her eating disorder they certainly left an impression and didn't help her self-esteem. The first time she weighed herself was when she was 13. She told her mum whose reaction was one of shock:

"You're X stone?! That much?! Oh, my Goodness!". This made her feel that it was something to be ashamed of. Throughout her childhood she was always referred to as having a big appetite and for being big. She says that this felt like how people defined her: "I would go round to a friend's house and their parents would say, 'I've given you extra because I have heard you're quite the gannet.' It was always mentioned if we went out to eat or if I was introduced to someone new. It began to feel like part of my identity. The constant references to being 'big' felt like people didn't know or care about 'me' as such, just the outside obvious things and that frustrated me." When she was 12, she clearly remembers her home economics teacher introducing the concept of "good" and "bad" foods during a healthy eating project. "To someone who is a perfectionist and has a strong desire to do right all the time, this wasn't the right wording! Categorizing foods like this started the beginning of the end for me."

Elena, 51, has suffered episodes of anorexia and bulimia since she was 18. She says: "From an early age I remember my mum always on the scales and then asking if she looked as if she had put on weight." She says her mum was always commenting on the appearance of others and she felt like the "heavy" one compared to her two sisters. "When I was 17 I lost weight and it felt like people noticed me for the first time. Being thin seemed to be the answer. My mum told me I looked better as my face was slimmer. I tried hard to maintain this image through bingeing, purging and restricting." Elena expresses her views with regards to how we talk to children: "I have very strong views about the way in which children must be given confidence from a very young age because it makes such a positive outcome for the future. The importance of growing up with a sense of worth is so essential. I now listen to comments like how fat my nephew is, or that the other nephew has slimmed down. It's all very disturbing to listen to. All the main comments to children are still about food and looks." Elena says that she is still searching for compassion toward herself and still struggles with anorexia.

One lady in her thirties shared that her mother put her on a diet aged 7. She now feels angry at her for doing this and knows it is at the root of her still suffering from low self-esteem and developing bulimia.

Another lady in her fifties was taken to the doctors aged 12 by her mother to see if they could do something to reduce the size of her legs. Her mum thought her legs spoiled her as she had a pretty face. She developed bulimia in her teens and still to this day does not show her legs. She has never worn a skirt.

A woman in her twenties was sent to Weight Watchers aged 7. She felt ashamed and went on to develop bulimia.

Another said that her mother had saved up money for her wedding but said she would rather she spent it on a gastric band. She said she had never felt accepted by her parents because she felt too fat; this just confirmed it. She developed bulimia as a teenager.

Another was told when she was 13 to batter her bum off the wall a hundred times a day because it was too big. She says she has always felt too fat and still struggles with binge eating.

One woman describes how her mother always made comments about her sister's body – "If only we all looked like that"; "She's so lucky to be so lovely and slim." She said there was constant references to her sister's "lovely slim body". This woman began to control her food intake, desperately trying to be as slim as her sister. She suffered and eating disorder for 20 years until she got help.

These personal accounts draw attention to the long lasting and devastating consequences of being on the receiving end of body comments and growing up in a family environment hyper-focused on food and weight. Most of these women, to this day, still struggle with food, weight and body image. It is evident that the common theme within all of these women's upbringings went on to have a profound negative effect on their lives.

What the Research Shows

Let's now connect those heartbreaking experiences with the compelling evidence from research and studies to shed further light on society's troubling reality.

There is a mountain of research that points to the fact that children raised in families hyper-focused on weight, food and body image, who are victims of teasing, having their body size criticized or it being suggested that they should lose weight, are at a heightened risk of developing negative body image and falling prey to eating disorders. A study in 2005 found that:

"Receiving comments of this nature from parents is associated with disordered eating which increases the risk for developing a full threshold eating disorder."[16]

One study revealed that when adults avoid making direct comments about their child's body but instead focus on making remarks about their own bodies, it can still exert a detrimental influence.

"… Well-meaning adults who purposely avoid commenting on their children's appearance may not realize the harm they are doing by talking about their own appearance. By modelling beliefs and behaviours relating to their own dissatisfaction with their body (e.g., criticizing their body, engaging in dieting/excessive exercise to lose weight), they can indirectly influence young people's body image and eating behaviours."[17]

Another study conducted in 2018 revealed the following:

"By witnessing her mother constantly criticizing her own body and engaging in diets and other weight loss strategies, a daughter may 'learn' that thinness is important. This may lead her to feel bad about her own appearance and then start copying her mother's behaviour, such as limiting how much food she eats, frequently weighing herself, and constantly checking her appearance in the mirror. This example of maternal modelling has been found in girls as young as 8 [years old]."[18]

A study carried out by the Journal of the American Dietetic Association showed that girls aged 5 had ideas and beliefs about dieting which they had learned from a member of their family.

"Girls whose mothers reported current or recent dieting were more than twice as likely to have ideas about dieting."[19]

The Journal of Abnormal Psychology's study showed that mothers' own dieting and eating problems were linked to their daughters' dieting and eating problems[20] and research carried out by the British Journal of Clinical Psychology found that mothers play a central role in transmitting cultural values regarding weight, shape, and appearance to daughters.[21] This research highlights the significant influence that adults wield in shaping children's body image and attitudes toward food.

My own personal experience aligns with these findings. I, too, was exposed to such messaging from a young age, and regrettably, like the women who have bravely shared their stories, also went on to struggle with an eating disorder.

The Complexities of Eating Disorders

It is crucial to emphasize at this point that while remarks and statements made either directly or indirectly during childhood about food, diets and body sizes can be extremely damaging, they are most likely not the *sole cause* of the development of an eating disorder. Eating disorders are extremely serious and complex mental illnesses and are often triggered by several factors. The causes are multifaceted, stemming from a blend of genetic, psychological, societal and environmental factors.

However, it is worth remembering that comments may undeniably plant a seed early on in life. They have the potential to prompt initial reflections on food and body size, amplifying existing insecurities. A focus on food and weight might serve as a channel for seeking control or for numbing distressing emotions, functioning as a coping mechanism. The seed that is planted early in childhood is often nurtured and grows when other aspects of life become overwhelming and beyond your control.

Hope For the Next Generation

"As a child I never heard one woman say to me, 'I love my body'. Not my mother, my elder sister, my best friend. No one woman has ever said, 'I am so proud of my body'. So I make sure to say it to Mia, my daughter, because a positive physical outlook has to start at an early age."[22]
Kate Winslet, actor

I am with Kate Winslet on this one. Our children deserve a different journey. It is of utmost importance for us to comprehend and be fully aware of the conscious and subconscious programming that affects children. Otherwise, the cycle will persist, and our daughters will pass these influences on to their daughters, just as our mothers did to us, and their mothers before them. The origins of this cycle may stretch back through generations, and it is our responsibility to break this chain for the wellbeing of future generations. We must make it known to our children that it is safe for everybody to exist in every type of body.

We know that children today already encounter immense pressure to conform to societal standards, bombarded from all sides. When they are also exposed to diet culture within their own homes, their vulnerability increases significantly. Without significant changes, they will be poised to inherit the legacy of self-loathing from their elders, perpetuating yet another generation destined to endure the same plight: grappling with body dissatisfaction and food-related struggles.

The harmful belief systems surrounding body image in my family have endured for at least four documented generations. I have distinct recollections of comments made by my grandmother during my childhood. It's evident that she grew up in an environment where the ideal of "being thin" held paramount importance. She often spoke of how her grandmother's body was bound to make it appear smaller and how they had to wear corsets that caused extreme pain and discomfort. She was hospitalized as a teenager in the 1920s for her refusal to eat, with her entire family pleading by her bedside, urging her to eat to avoid dire consequences. This occurred decades before anorexia nervosa found its place in the Diagnostic and Statistical Manual of Mental Disorders (DSM) as a recognized psychological disorder. Throughout my childhood, I absorbed and internalized my family's deep rooted body image beliefs. The sheer volume of messages with reference to food, weight and body size that I was exposed to undoubtedly led to my body image struggles and it also seems like I may have been genetically predisposed.

Studies indicate that dieting significantly contributes to the emergence of eating disorders. It is reported that one in four who diet will go on to develop an eating disorder and it's a widely recognized fact that when parents engage in dieting, their children are more inclined to adopt the same behaviours.

As responsible adults, we must ask ourselves the following questions:

- Would we wish for our children to spend their lives consumed by body size concerns or worrying about their food intake?
- Do we want to subject our children to the potential risks of developing an eating disorder?

Given the rising rates of eating disorders and body dissatisfaction, it is crucial that we understand how children interpret the messages they receive from their elders about food and body image, and to consider how these messages can be optimized to promote positive outcomes for children's physical and mental health.

What Can We Do?

As this chapter concludes, it is fundamental to reiterate that its purpose is not to assign blame. We are all entrenched in a culture fixated on body size, and we are all impacted by it. Commenting on bodies, including our own, others' and our children's, is unfortunately considered the norm in our society. We are all a product of our upbringing. However, we have the power to choose differently. Both the research findings and first-hand accounts point to the fact that a thorough reassessment of the language we employ regarding food, weight and body image in front of children is imperative. We can make a conscious decision, starting from this moment on, not to participate in this harmful behaviour.

One effective approach to reshape a child's perception of food and their body is to be mindful of the language you use regarding your own body, your child's body, or anyone's body. Minimizing the emphasis on food can also be beneficial. In fact, the most impactful strategy may be to refrain from saying anything at all on these matters. The next time you feel compelled to comment on a child's body or size, refrain from doing so. The next time you find yourself tempted to discuss someone else's body or criticize your own, hold back. Take a moment to pause the next time you are about to make a remark about someone's eating habits. How about from this moment on you take the lead in challenging the status quo. Be the person in your family who advocates for the idea that being healthy is not always synonymous with being "thin". Be the bold individual who stands apart from the crowd for the sake of the next generation.

By the simple act of saying nothing, you can contribute to breaking the cycle of negative body image that is perpetuated from one generation to the next. Our words and actions carry profound weight and can have both constructive and devastating consequences. We have the power to proactively bring about change that can have an enormous positive impact on future generations. Let's make sure we address this as a matter of urgency.

As we confront the perils of diet culture within our homes and the lasting impact of our words, the path ahead beckons us to confront the consequences of suffering from a negative body image. In the chapters that follow, we delve deeper into this pressing issue, illuminating the importance of fostering a more positive and nurturing environment for the next generation. Together, we can journey toward a brighter future where our children can grow with confidence and self-love.

5

THE DANGERS OF NEGATIVE BODY IMAGE

In this chapter, we embark on a deep exploration of the harrowing journey of dealing with a negative body image – a battle that I have fought first-hand. The following pages will unravel the intricate web of consequences that can ensnare individuals caught in the grip of this ingrained issue. From its insidious impact on mental health, plunging individuals into the depths of depression and anxiety, to the strains it places on personal relationships, this chapter offers an intimate look into the profound and often devastating aftermath of a negative body image. It serves as a stark reminder of why we must do everything possible to attempt to break the negative body image cycle for our children.

In this chapter I candidly recount my personal journey of grappling with a negative body image, which resulted in persistent feelings of inadequacy, depression and the development of an eating disorder. Moreover, this affliction profoundly influenced my social interactions and relationships.

Negative body image, prevalent across various demographics but notably affecting women, involves a distorted self-perception of body shape and size. It takes a toll on both mental and physical wellbeing, resulting in consequences like low self-esteem, heightened anxiety and depression. Furthermore, it can trigger harmful behaviours such as disordered eating, body dysmorphia, substance abuse, or even self-harm. The ramifications of suffering from poor body image ripple through every facet of one's life.

Let's delve deeper into how negative body image intricately weaves its impact into one's life and dissect it piece by piece.

Negative Body Image and Low Self Esteem

Negative body image and low self-esteem are intertwined issues with profound implications for mental health and overall wellbeing. This self-destructive cycle is fuelled by constant self-criticism, social comparisons, avoidance and isolation, as well as mood and mental health challenges. It also casts a shadow over personal relationships and can lead to harmful coping mechanisms, such as disordered eating or substance abuse.

I personally resonate with connection between suffering from a negative body image and low self-esteem. I battled incessant self-criticism primarily centred on my appearance. I felt inadequate and harboured intense hatred for my own body, which took a severe toll on my self-esteem. I habitually engaged in comparisons with various people – friends, members of my family, random strangers, actors or popstars. This only intensified the negative emotions I felt about my body and had a detrimental impact on my self-worth. It took years of work to gradually build up my self-esteem.

Negative Body Image and Anxiety

Suffering from anxiety and having a negative body image are often interconnected, with one exacerbating the other. Individuals who struggle with negative body image may experience anxiety around social situations, such as going on holiday or participating in physical activities, for fear of being judged or ridiculed for their appearance. This anxiety can lead to avoidance behaviours and social isolation, which in turn can further reinforce negative body image. Moreover, anxiety can also fuel unhealthy coping mechanisms, such as emotional eating or substance abuse, which can have a detrimental impact on both mental and physical health.

As previously discussed, the anxiety I grappled with due to body image concerns had a significant ripple effect on my social life. The fear of exposing my body, whether in a swimsuit or during certain activities, proved too daunting to bear – the anxiety was overwhelming and ultimately lead me to opt for avoidance as my primary coping strategy. The anxiety was heightened at the thought of going shopping, trying on clothes or attending special events like weddings or nights out. On an average day as a teenager, I recall consistently experiencing heightened anxiety while wearing my school uniform, primarily due to an overwhelming fear of judgment regarding my body size.

Negative Body Image and Depression

Depression and negative body image often coexist, with one influencing the other. Individuals who struggle with negative body image may experience feelings of hopelessness and low self-esteem. Negative thoughts related to the body can lead to a vicious cycle of self-doubt, where one's perception of their body becomes increasingly distorted, and they may feel like they are trapped in a never-ending cycle of self-criticism. Furthermore, the effects of depression on energy levels, motivation and overall wellbeing can make it difficult to engage in healthy behaviours, such as exercise and proper nutrition, which can further exacerbate negative body image.

I battled clinical depression alongside my enduring struggle with negative body image, though I didn't recognize this until later in my therapeutic journey when I became more self-aware. I can vividly recall the profound sense of unworthiness that once plagued me.

Negative Body Image and Eating Disorders

Suffering from negative body image often leads to disordered eating as individuals try to conform to societal beauty standards to deal with overwhelming emotions and to achieve a certain body shape or size. Restrictive dieting and an obsessive focus on food and weight can trigger disordered eating patterns and a loss of control over one's relationship with food. We know that dieting is a main contributor to the development of eating disorders such as bulimia nervosa, binge eating disorder, anorexia nervosa and others. If left untreated, eating disorders can have serious physical and mental health consequences.

Eating disorders centre on extreme concerns about weight, size, shape of the body and food intake. They are characterized by obsessive thoughts that your body or parts of your body are severely flawed. Sufferers will go to extreme measures to try and hide their body or to try and fix it by engaging in dangerous behaviours with food and punishing exercise regimes. Most sufferers will feel extreme self-consciousness and wholly despise the image that stares back at them in the mirror.

All eating disorders affect every area of a person's life – emotionally, physically and socially. It is hard for sufferers to escape the negative feelings and thoughts that bombard their minds incessantly. They can't escape their body or the thoughts they have about it and become stuck in a vicious cycle of negative thoughts and behaviours. Loathing every inch of your body is a huge part of suffering from an eating disorder.

I fully resonate with this – I engaged in behaviours like dieting, calorie checking, daily weighing, skipping meals, bingeing on food, constant comparison, feeling guilt after eating, pushing myself to the point of exhaustion with punishing exercise routines, constantly body checking in mirrors and reflections, and taking various diuretics to enable weight loss. I lived what I thought at the time was a normal life with rigid rules around food and exercise; I missed out on life experiences due to body image concerns and wasted years striving for a body type that was unattainable for my genetic makeup.

Binge Eating Disorder

Binge eating disorder – the most common eating disorder – is strongly linked to negative body image. People with binge eating disorder often have a distorted perception of their body and may experience significant shame and guilt about their eating behaviours, leading to negative self-image. The experience of binge eating itself can exacerbate negative body image, as individuals may feel out of control and disgusted with themselves after an episode. The cycle of bingeing and negative self-talk can further fuel negative body image, leading to a vicious cycle of low self-esteem and unhealthy behaviours. The shame and secrecy associated with binge eating disorder can also lead individuals to avoid social situations or engage in hiding behaviours, further exacerbating negative body image and social isolation. Overall, the link between binge eating disorder and negative body image is a complex one, highlighting the importance of comprehensive support and treatment for individuals struggling with these issues.

Bulimia Nervosa

Bulimia nervosa is an eating disorder characterized by binge eating followed by purging behaviours such as self-induced vomiting or the use of diuretics, strict dieting or over-exercising. It often starts with a fixation on shape, weight and size as a way of dealing with overwhelming emotions. People with bulimia nervosa often have an intense fear of gaining weight and feel a loss of control over their eating habits.

Engaging in bulimic behaviours can lead to many health problems such as dental issues, organ complications, digestive disorders, irregular heartbeat, heart failure, electrolyte imbalance, fatigue, anxiety and depression. Suffering from bulimia nervosa is difficult to overcome without professional help. Treatment involves a combination of therapy, medication and nutritional counselling to help individuals develop a healthier relationship with food and their body.

Anorexia Nervosa

Anorexia nervosa is the least common but the most serious eating disorder with the highest mortality rate of any mental illness. It is characterized by a distorted perception of body weight and shape, an intense fear of gaining weight, and a persistent restriction of food intake. Although in some cases sufferers become extremely underweight, it is not always the case. An individual can be suffering from anorexia in a body of any size.

Individuals with anorexia nervosa often have a distorted self-image and view themselves as overweight, even if they are underweight. Their negative body image is often exacerbated by social pressures to conform to a particular body type and can lead to extreme weight loss and malnourishment. Some sufferers will examine their bodies several times a day, check their weight and size obsessively and base their whole self-worth on the size of their body.

The physical and psychological consequences of anorexia nervosa can be severe: cardiac complications, organ failure, anaemia, fertility problems, osteoporosis, anxiety, depression and even suicide. Without proper treatment, the disorder can be life-threatening. Treatment for anorexia nervosa often involves a combination of psychotherapy, medication and nutritional counselling.

It is important to be aware that eating disorders can affect anyone of any age, sex, size, religion and race. They do not discriminate. Suffering from an eating disorder is not just fussy eating and it is not a phase: people don't grow out of an eating disorder. All eating disorders are serious mental health illnesses.

Negative Body Image and Body Dysmorphic Disorder

Body dysmorphia, also known as body dysmorphic disorder (BDD), is a mental health condition where an individual has a persistent and obsessive preoccupation with perceived flaws or defects in their physical appearance that are not noticeable to others or are minor in nature. People with body dysmorphia often experience significant distress and impairment in their daily lives due to their negative body image, and they may engage in compulsive behaviours such as excessive grooming, the constant seeking of reassurance or engaging in cosmetic procedures.

Negative Body Image and Social Life

Suffering with negative body image can have a significant impact on one's social life. People who have a negative perception of their body are often self-conscious and may feel uncomfortable in social situations, leading them to withdraw from social events and avoid meeting new people. They may also feel like they don't fit in or belong, which can lead to feelings of isolation and loneliness. Negative body image can also lead to social anxiety, making it challenging to interact with others and form meaningful relationships. In extreme cases, negative body image can even lead to social phobia, which can severely impact one's ability to function in social settings.

What should be enjoyable occasions, like attending weddings or social gatherings, can turn into sources of anxiety and unease for individuals grappling with negative body image. They anticipate experiencing self-loathing, regardless of their choice of attire, which can make such events seem daunting. Avoiding these situations may sometimes appear as an easier alternative.

Even shopping can become a distressing experience, as individuals tend to fixate on perceived flaws and imperfections in their bodies. Activities like going swimming or holidaying in places where more skin exposure is expected can also be highly intimidating, as they involve a level of self-exposure that may trigger significant anxiety.

I can deeply relate to this, as I once went to great lengths to avoid any situation that heightened my negative body image. On those rare occasions when I did summon the courage to attend events like weddings, the experience was marred because I couldn't fully immerse myself in the moment or engage with others. My thoughts were constantly consumed by how my body appeared, overshadowing the joyous occasion.

Negative Body Image and Substance Abuse

Substance abuse and negative body image can be linked in several ways. For instance, some individuals may turn to substances as a means of coping with the negative emotions that stem from their negative body image (for example, low self-esteem, anxiety and depression). The use of substances as a coping mechanism can become habitual and lead to addiction. Additionally, substance abuse can have physical effects on the body, such as changes in weight, skin conditions and other changes in appearance, which can further impact one's negative body image. This may create a vicious cycle, as individuals use substances to cope with their negative emotions related to the body dissatisfaction that has resulted from their substance abuse.

I discovered alcohol at the age of 14, and it seemed like a solution to my problems. It provided temporary relief from the overwhelming thoughts and emotions tied to my body image issues, which unfortunately led to irresponsible use. This pattern only intensified my ongoing internal struggle.

Negative Body Image and Self-Harm

For some individuals, the negative feelings of body dissatisfaction, shame and self-consciousness can lead to self-harm behaviours such as cutting, burning or hitting oneself. Self-harm can serve as a coping mechanism for dealing with intense emotions or feelings of self-hatred.

Seeking professional help is crucial for individuals struggling with these issues. Therapy, medication and support from loved ones can all be beneficial in improving body image and reducing the urge to self-harm.

Negative Body Image and Relationships

Negative body image can have a detrimental impact on relationships. People who have a negative perception of their body may struggle with self-confidence, which can affect their ability to form and maintain relationships. They may feel unworthy of love and attention, leading them to distance themselves from others or sabotage their relationships. In addition, negative body image can cause individuals to project their insecurities onto their partners, leading to mistrust, jealousy and other relationship issues. This can be especially problematic in intimate relationships, where vulnerability and trust are essential. Negative body image can also lead to a lack of intimacy and decreased sexual satisfaction, as individuals may feel uncomfortable or self-conscious during intimate moments.

My negative body image had a significant impact on my relationships. I vehemently despised every part of my body, which made it challenging for others to express their affection for parts of me that I regarded as repulsive.

The Effects Run Deep

Suffering with negative body image, coupled with what I suspect to have been body dysmorphic disorder (though never formally diagnosed), had a profound and devastating impact on my life. It was a destructive cycle of negativity, resulting in depression, anxiety, low self-esteem, substance abuse and an eating disorder. My initial coping mechanism was through dieting, which eventually spiralled into an eating disorder. By the age of 14, I had turned to alcohol as a means of escape from my emotional pain. It was only through therapy that I found the path to healing and began the process of rebuilding my fragile self-esteem.

In conclusion, the profound and far-reaching repercussions of a negative body image are undeniable. It can have a significant impact on an individual's mental health and wellbeing, affecting their confidence, relationships and overall quality of life. Its impact can be pervasive and debilitating.

In our society, it's a rarity to come across someone content with their appearance, as our bodies frequently shape our self-identity. Consequently, grappling with negative body image and engaging in an ongoing internal struggle can seem almost second nature. Despite the messages conveyed by the media and others it is crucial to acknowledge that constantly feeling negative about one's body is not a healthy or normal state. Of course, it is natural to sometimes have concerns about one's appearance or to desire changes to the shape of one's body, and to experience occasional self-consciousness – but this should never be at the expense of your health. The thoughts and feelings and behaviours centred toward your body should not consume your daily life or negatively impact your mental and emotional wellbeing. If they are disrupting your daily life, it's crucial to recognize that seeking professional assistance becomes essential.

In this chapter we have examined every facet of the suffering caused by a negative body image, emphasizing its profound and enduring consequences. It exerts a considerable influence on an individual's life potentially paving the way for severe mental health disorders like bulimia nervosa and anorexia nervosa, as well as depression and anxiety. Furthermore, we've underscored its far-reaching effects on an individual's social and personal life.

Recognizing the significance of this issue underscores the importance of fostering a positive body image, seeking support when needed, and embarking on a path toward self-acceptance. By embarking on a journey to cultivate a positive body image and emphasizing overall health and wellbeing, individuals can enhance their quality of life and lead happier, healthier lives as well as changing the narrative for the next generation. The upcoming chapter will propose strategies to improve one's body image.

6

HOW TO IMPROVE BODY IMAGE

Enhancing one's body image demands a comprehensive and ongoing approach. It's a journey peppered with peaks and troughs, requiring self-reflection, continuous learning and a candid examination of our insecurities. The process involves the deliberate unlearning of biased beliefs regarding physical appearance, empowering us to cultivate confidence in our bodies. This is a deeply personal responsibility that no one else can undertake on our behalf.

It is of utmost importance to identify and confront all the factors that trigger distress and foster destructive thoughts and behaviours. If you are committed to putting in the effort, the ability to attain authentic peace with your body and your relationship with food lies well within your grasp. You possess the capacity to break free from the relentless cycle of body- and food-related challenges, not only within yourself but also within your family and broader society. By choosing to challenge societal norms, you become a catalyst for meaningful change.

In chapters 2 and 3, we explored the intricate formation of our body image, investigating the profound impact of external influences on our perceptions and behaviours concerning our physical selves. Understanding the origins of our beliefs about our bodies and recognizing the ways societal pressures have shaped our thoughts and actions can be a pivotal step toward initiating transformative and constructive shifts in our perspective and approach.

We understand that our body image evolves gradually, influenced by a range of personal experiences and external factors, some of which are positive, while others are negative. It is undeniable that many of us have been subjected to conditioning that fosters a negative perception of our bodies. The origins of this suffering from a negative body image are deeply rooted and nurtured by a variety of oppressive forces that affect us all.

Breaking the entrenched link between thinness and happiness is a complex task, particularly in a society that relentlessly reinforces the notion that thinness is the ultimate solution to all problems. The pervasive presence of diet culture and the prevalence of fat phobia infiltrate every aspect of our lives, from our homes and educational systems to healthcare, politics, the entertainment industry and the media. Disordered eating behaviours are often promoted and normalized, perpetuating the cycle of negative body image and its associated challenges.

Glennon Doyle hits the nail on the head in her outstanding book *Untamed*:

"We must try and rid ourselves of this poison, it is difficult for a woman to be healthy in a culture that is still so very sick."[23]

The purpose of this chapter is to lead you in the direction of liberating yourself from the constraints of diet culture and embarking on a transformative journey toward undoing the years of societal conditioning you have experienced. It proposes simple techniques to help you break the cycle of self-loathing. Its primary objective is to propel you toward a new journey of self-discovery that involves accepting yourself and appreciating your body in a revolutionary way. By encouraging you to reconsider your thought processes, behaviours, relationships with others and with the media, this chapter will motivate you to challenge cultural beliefs about the "ideal" body type.

The Beginning of Your Journey

To gain a deeper understanding of the journey ahead, take a moment to contemplate the following suggestions:

• Can you picture a life free from a constant, negative inner monologue concerning your body and food?
• Can you imagine a life free from dieting?
• Can you imagine eating intuitively like how you did as a baby – eating when hungry and stopping when full?
• Can you imagine looking in the mirror and liking what you see?
• Can you imagine never weighing yourself again?
• Can you imagine ordering what you truly desire from a menu?
• Can you imagine exercising solely for the pleasure it brings?
• Can you imagine how it would it feel to live a life where you genuinely like and accept yourself, free from the daily thought of "I need to lose weight"?
• Do you envision the possibility of being able to compliment yourself in the same manner as you would a friend?
• Can you fathom the sense of freedom, peace and joy that would come with such a life?

As you embark on this journey, it is of utmost importance to acknowledge that patience is paramount. The transition from body-loathing to body-acceptance is a gradual process that demands time. Unravelling deeply ingrained beliefs imposed upon us by diet culture and societal norms surrounding our bodies and food cannot be accomplished in a matter of weeks. If you have invested decades of effort in attempts to change your body, the concept of acceptance may seem unfamiliar and might even give the impression of neglecting your health. It's important to clarify that being healthy doesn't equate to a specific body size. However, discerning the initial steps toward this mindset can indeed be challenging.

Here are some initial recommendations to kickstart your journey toward positive body image:

- **Practise self-compassion**. Treating yourself with kindness, understanding and acceptance – especially during times of difficulty – is crucial.
- **Challenge thinking patterns**. Being aware of persistent negative self-chatter is of paramount importance.
- **Use positive affirmations**. Integrating empowering affirmations into your daily routine strengthens self-confidence and self-belief.
- **Challenge behaviours**. Being mindful of your actions is vital if you aim to bring about meaningful transformations.
- **Reject diet culture**. Engaging with literature and social media content that explores the subject is important to help expand your knowledge and enhance your comprehension.
- **Challenge what you see in the media**. Thoroughly comprehending and critically evaluating the continuous influx of media messages to which you are exposed is critical.
- **Focus on body function**. Gaining an insight into the functioning of your body is key, helping you to see your body in a completely different way.
- **Practise body gratitude**. Expressing gratitude toward your body for the way it functions and its abilities will help you improve body image.

- **Celebrate your achievements**. Recognizing and honouring all your achievements, big or small, and taking pride in the progress you've made helps to improve self-worth.
- **Enjoy joyful movement**. Choosing physical activities that bring you joy rather than viewing them as a punishment or an obligation is an invaluable step to take.
- **Wear clothes that fit**. Opting for clothing that allows you to feel at ease and confident and comfortable in your own skin is pivotal.
- **Be around those who are supportive**. Being around people who are likeminded is fundamental.
- **Be aware of all your triggers**. Self-awareness plays a vital role in the process of understanding what triggers you to feel bad about your body.
- **Feel your emotions**. Allowing yourself to feel emotions that are suppressed is key on this journey.

Let's explore these suggestions.

Practise Self-Compassion

Prioritizing self-compassion and extending to yourself the same kindness you readily offer others is essential when striving to enhance your body image. A practical starting point involves integrating activities that uplift and nurture you, even if it means dedicating just five minutes each day.

Here are a few simple and practical self-care suggestions to get you started:

- Have a bath
- Listen to a podcast
- Do a breathing exercise
- Book a massage

- Go for a walk-in nature
- Read
- Do something creative
- Write a letter
- Do a meditation
- Get to a yoga class
- Put on a facemask
- Go for a coffee
- Journal your thoughts

Carving out time for yourself daily may pose challenges, especially if you have work responsibilities, run a household or have children to attend to. Initially, prioritizing self-care might feel unfamiliar, but it's a skill that can be cultivated with effort.

On a personal level, it took some time for me to fully adopt this practice. Initially, I had to intentionally make time for myself, but over time, it has integrated into my routine. Today, I effortlessly set aside moments each day solely for my own wellbeing, free from any sense of guilt.

Self-compassion is also granting yourself forgiveness for harbouring hatred toward your body. It involves understanding that neither you nor the people who instilled these beliefs are to blame if your goal has always been to "get thin". It is perfectly normal that this has been your focus. From early childhood, you have likely associated being "thin" with love, acceptance, respect, attention and success – core elements necessary for survival. You most likely have been exposed to damaging messages about what constitutes a "worthy" body, and diet culture has instilled in you numerous beliefs that have eroded your connection with your body, food and exercise.

Perhaps now is the moment to cease criticizing yourself for not meeting societal expectations and instead embrace a more compassionate approach toward yourself. Being gentler with yourself in all situations – whether within the family, at work, with friends or to do with body image – is of paramount importance.

Challenge Thinking Patterns

The power that our thoughts have to cause significant harm becomes apparent when we begin to recognize and confront them. This process can be a deeply challenging one. Prior to seeking therapy, I had no realization of the profoundly destructive nature of my thoughts. It was only through therapy that I became aware of the sheer volume of negative thoughts that occupied my mind each day. These thoughts had become my normality, surfacing automatically, and consuming my thinking process obsessively. They proved to be unhelpful and relentlessly wore me down. Therapy played a pivotal role in enabling me to recognize the detrimental impact of these thoughts and taught me how to challenge my destructive thinking patterns.

Perhaps you have not yet fully grasped the extent of your thoughts and their influence on you. A preliminary step could involve unravelling your current relationship with your thoughts. Begin by paying closer attention to your internal dialogue. Take notice of the thoughts that arise when you observe yourself in the mirror. Observe the thoughts that precede and follow your meals. Observe the thoughts that arise when you engage in physical activity or when you are unable to exercise. Become mindful of all the inner chatter that occurs within you.

Embracing the habit of journaling your daily thoughts about food, your body and your overall self can be beneficial. Allocate some time to evaluate the nature of these thoughts, distinguishing between those that are constructive and those that are hindering you. Honesty with yourself is paramount in this process. Take note of whether most of your thoughts tend to lean toward negativity or positivity, then delve deeper into their origins.

Consider whether societal conditioning plays a role in shaping these thoughts. Reflect on whether they surface automatically or if you possess conscious control over them. Challenge them by seeking evidence that supports or refutes their validity. This reflective practice empowers you to better understand and address the cognitive thinking patterns that influence your body image.

Allow me to provide a couple of relatable examples.

Picture yourself catching your reflection in a mirror or a shop window, and almost instinctively, you utter self-critical remarks such as "What a state", "Fat bitch" or "You're so fat". These thoughts immediately trigger a cascade of negative dialogue in your mind. You find yourself thinking, "I must exercise more", "I wish I hadn't had that second helping" or "I need to stick to this diet." Before you know it, this internal dialogue has taken over your mind, consuming your thoughts incessantly.

An effective technique worth attempting is to challenge each thought that arises and flip it. Take notice of the thought, and consciously replace it with more positive and compassionate words and statements.

Consciously replace, "What a state" or "Fat bitch" with "I am unique" or "I am more than just my appearance." Rather than, "You look terrible in that dress" or "Your legs are too big in those jeans", consider "I feel confident and comfortable in what I'm wearing" or "My body is strong and capable." Substitute thoughts like "I must do more exercise" or "I need to stick to this diet" with "I choose to engage in activities that nourish and energize my body" or "I prioritize my wellbeing through balanced and mindful choices."

While this task may initially feel daunting, with daily practice and the incorporation of the "flip the thought" mantra, it can transform into an enjoyable game you play with yourself. It does take effort and dedication – however, over time, as has happened in my case, it becomes a habit that empowers you to shift your internal chatter in a kinder and more uplifting direction.

Use Positive Affirmations

Over two decades ago, during a therapy session, I received invaluable guidance that has remained a steadfast companion on my journey. It was a simple yet profound recommendation: for every negative self-comment I uttered, I should counter it with ten positive affirmations. At that juncture in my life, my self-esteem and self-worth were nearly non-existent. Initially, I found it challenging to wholeheartedly embrace these alternative, more nurturing affirmations. However, I consciously chose to place my trust in the process and persevere.

Day after day, I diligently recited these affirmations, determined to drown out the cacophony of negative inner dialogue. Slowly, but steadily, I began to internalize and absorb them, and I noticed a positive shift in how I perceived myself. The unwavering commitment to replacing negativity with positivity played a pivotal role in rebuilding my self-esteem, transforming it from a fragile state to one of resilience and self-assuredness.

Feel free to create your own personalized affirmations that resonate with you to help provide a positive shift in your mindset. Here are a few suggestions:

- I am a good friend.
- I am worthy at any size.
- I am kind.
- I am good at my job.
- I am good at drawing.
- I am hardworking.
- I am thoughtful.

The success of this exercise ultimately depends on the amount of effort, work and time you are willing to invest in it. One simple perspective to adopt is to ask yourself whether you would say the same unkind things to a friend. It goes back to the practice of self-compassion. If the answer is no, then it is unacceptable to speak to yourself in that manner.

Learning to drown out negative thoughts and replace them with kinder, more compassionate ones is an achievable goal for everyone. The key lies in being aware of the negative self-chatter and actively working on changing it. If you find that your thoughts are overwhelming or persistent, it may be beneficial to seek professional help. Cognitive Behavioural Therapy (CBT) can assist in sorting out and recognizing deep-rooted thought patterns and behaviours, providing valuable guidance in the process of transformation.

Challenge Behaviours

While it's completely natural to take pride in your appearance, prioritize exercise and seek nourishing food for your body, it's important to reflect on the extent to which these pursuits contribute to your overall wellbeing. A first step is to recognize and become aware of what actions and behaviours you have in a day that are related to your food intake and changing your body.

I was completely unaware of the extent to which my behaviours were obsessively detrimental to my wellbeing until I began therapy. Weighing myself, bodychecking and dieting had become obsessive habits. It hadn't occurred to me that incessantly scrutinizing my body, counting calories and feeling guilty about every bite of food, or weighing myself multiple times a day were profoundly unhealthy practices. Seeking professional help played a significant role in helping me acknowledge and subsequently confront these unhealthy behaviours. Through therapy, I learned to recognize and challenge harmful behavioural patterns, with a significantly positive effect.

Getting rid of bathroom scales played a pivotal role in my journey. It became imperative for me to reach a realization that my worth transcended mere numbers. It took considerable time and extensive therapy for me to internalize the notion that a piece of metal only revealed my gravitational force within this vast universe, while failing to capture any of my individual accomplishments or intrinsic qualities. With great pride, I can confidently declare that I have not entertained the thought of stepping onto a scale for over 25 years.

Mirror checking and body checking can also manifest as obsessive behaviours. Take notice of how frequently you engage in doing this. Challenge yourself to abstain from looking in mirrors or fixating on specific body parts for an entire day. This potentially destructive habit *can* be broken with heightened awareness. During therapy, I reached a point where I was advised to remove all mirrors from my house for a while. Doing so proved instrumental in breaking the cycle.

If daily weighing, dieting or body checking are persistent focuses for you, deeply ingrained due to upbringing, seeking professional assistance might be instrumental to help breaking this cycle.

Reject Diet Culture

Abandoning the practice of dieting is a fundamental step toward enhancing body image. Releasing the diet mentality and behaviours is a transformative process that demands considerable effort and inner self-work. Initially, breaking free from this mindset can feel strange, especially if you have been a dieter your entire life.

Many individuals who have spent their lives following restrictive diets can attest to the fact that as soon as they embark on a diet, they find themselves fixating on the foods they are prohibited from having, thus disconnecting from their natural hunger and fullness cues, and generating intense cravings. What you deny yourself becomes the object of obsession.

Embracing a diet-culture-free lifestyle involves allowing yourself to enjoy a wide range of foods while fostering a deep sense of trust and respect for your body. It's crucial to remember that as a baby and child, you were naturally in tune with your body's signals until societal diet norms interfered, instilling doubt in your body's wisdom. The possibility exists for you to reconnect with that intuitive eater within, living a life free from fixation, regulations, limitations and restrictions. Evelyn Tribole and Elyse Resch's book titled *Intuitive Eating: A Revolutionary Anti-Diet Approach* is an invaluable guide to help you liberate yourself from the shackles of dieting. Your body possesses innate wisdom; it inherently understands its needs.

Challenge What You See In the Media

The notion that being thin equates to health and happiness has been deeply ingrained in our collective consciousness. It permeates our everyday language, our homes, workplaces, our social feeds, and even digital spaces like WhatsApp group chats. It manifests within the media, children's programmes and movies, supermarket aisles, our healthcare and education systems, as well as political structures.

How frequently do you come across images throughout your day that affect your body image? The underlying message from the media is that you must change your body, that you are not good enough the way you are.

Developing an awareness of diet culture's pervasive presence is crucial. To effectively challenge what you see in the media, it's important to examine all aspects of your life and identify where diet culture messaging infiltrates, with an understanding that it often disguises itself as wellness, fitness or wellbeing initiatives. Begin to consciously observe the messages that inundate your daily life, whether through social media, your commute or television consumed and uncover the hidden intentions – and who benefits from them.

One impactful strategy is to acknowledge that most bodies depicted in the media are far from reality. They are often airbrushed, digitally altered and manipulated to conform to society's idea of perfection. Perhaps it's time to actively challenge these representations. You could start by refusing to support these ideals – avoid purchasing trashy magazines, or call them out, expressing your discontent with their content on social media.

To enhance your body image, it's essential to critically evaluate the media content you consume. Consider unfollowing or clearing out any social media accounts that consistently make you feel negative about your self-esteem and self-worth. Additionally, seek out literature that promotes body positivity and follow relevant Instagram and Twitter accounts that advocate for diverse body types.

Focus On Body Function and Practise Gratitide

Embracing body appreciation is an exceptionally powerful strategy to combat negative body image. It's crucial to recognize that bodies encompass far more than mere appearances – they are not simply ornaments to be ogled and admired. Your body is a compassionate, intelligent and diligent companion that dutifully serves you every day with minimal effort.

For those fortunate individuals who have a fully functioning healthy body, each day, effortlessly and without your conscious input: your eyes see, your ears hear, your heart beats, your lungs enable you to breathe.

Once you acquire a fresh perspective on your body, it becomes increasingly effortless to cultivate kindness toward it, to foster a more positive outlook, to be thankful for its capabilities, and to genuinely value it for its functionality rather than its outward appearance.

Consider using the following positive affirmations to facilitate the process:

- *I appreciate my eyes as they let me take in nature.*
- *I appreciate my ears as they let me listen to my favourite songs or radio shows every day.*

- *I appreciate my legs as they are strong and allow me to walk to work every day.*
- *I appreciate my heart as it beats for me every day without any effort.*

You can create personalized affirmations tailored specifically to your own journey. This invaluable and uplifting tool has proven to be highly effective in fostering a positive body image and uplifting one's self-esteem.

Another enjoyable activity to consider is to create a positive body advert on some fun and colourful stationary, expressing gratitude for every small contribution your body makes, even those mysterious organs like your spleen. Keep it close and make a habit of reading it daily – on the bus, on the train, on the toilet, literally anywhere. Shower your body with the love and appreciation it deserves.

Consider reflecting on moments when you experienced physical pain or illness – during those times, you longed for better health and promised to never take it for granted again. However, once you recovered, those sentiments faded. You don't have to wait for your body to falter in order to appreciate it and yearn for good health. Start appreciating it now. Cultivate daily body gratitude and appreciation as a ritual. Place affirmations around your home or on mirrors as reminders. Each day, reflect on what your body does for you and express heartfelt gratitude.

Another beneficial exercise is to reflect on aspects of yourself that you genuinely like. I recall struggling with this exercise during therapy, finding it challenging to identify something I truly liked. It's okay to take it slow. Begin with small things like appreciating your nails, hands or hair, and gradually expand from there. Remember, even starting with something seemingly insignificant can serve as a foundation for building a more positive self-perception.

Learning to accept aspects of your body that you cannot change may be something you need to work on and may require some effort. Perhaps your wish to be taller, have different hair, or you believe your nose is too big. It's common to obsess over these perceived flaws and yearn for change. While loving every part of your body is not necessary, you can strive to accept the parts of your body that you can't change and avoid being overly critical of yourself. The key lies in acknowledging that we are all unique, and the very traits you consider imperfect are what make you unique.

I strongly encourage you to explore all the previously mentioned suggestions for improving your body image. However, it's important to remember that this journey is personal, and you have the freedom to tailor it to your unique needs and preferences.

I highly recommend delving into the book *More Than a Body: Your Body Is an Instrument, Not an Ornament* by Lexie and Lindsay Kite. This insightful read further reinforces the idea that your body should be viewed as a valuable instrument rather than a mere decoration.

Nothing positive ever comes from hating your body. Since you will be together for a lifetime, would it not be worthwhile to foster a friendship with your body rather than criticizing it for not conforming to certain standards? Why not shift your focus toward its functionality and marvel every day at its remarkable capabilities? Accepting that your body is not your enemy is of utmost importance. You can commit to investing the same level of energy into accepting your body as you invested in the pursuit of hating it.

Celebrate Your Achievements

Do you feel you consistently engage in self-criticism and fail to acknowledge your own accomplishments? Do you consistently underestimate your worth in all aspects of life, being excessively hard on yourself and rarely recognizing your successes in a positive light? Are you constantly focused on the next goal, disregarding the milestones you have already surpassed on your personal journey? You may simply find yourself consumed by the relentless demands of everyday life, losing sight of your own wellbeing.

The following suggestion may assist you in acknowledging and appreciating your life achievements.

Invest in some fun stationery and start jotting down all your life accomplishments, regardless of their perceived insignificance. Perhaps you emerged triumphant in your school sports competition, aced a spelling test, passed your driving test, wrote a song, got accepted at college or university, got a job, embraced parenthood, or gave a helping hand to a stranger. The contents of this list is entirely personal to you. Make a habit of referencing it daily.

This technique serves as an excellent means to cultivate self-esteem. You have accomplished remarkable feats, and it is crucial to remind yourself of these accomplishments. When engaging in this exercise the focus is so far removed from what your body looks like. It serves as a stark reminder that you are more than a body.

Enjoy Joyful Movement

While on a journey to improve body image it might be helpful to let go of the notion that the sole purpose of exercise is for punishment, weight loss and burning calories. So many of us push our bodies to the brink of exhaustion, engaging in brutal exercise regimes daily to burn off as many calories as possible, all-in pursuit of the "ideal body".

I'm not suggesting you should abstain from going to the gym or from participating in exercise classes if those activities bring you joy; my point is that exercise should not be about adhering to rigid rules and expectations. This is about encouraging you to engage in behaviours that make you feel good about your body and don't feel like a chore. Instead of subjecting yourself to intense workouts, why not explore gentler alternatives like yoga, taking leisurely walks, cycling amidst nature, or join a dance class. Find ways to move your body that bring you joy. Focus on engaging in activities that boost your body positivity. It's important to reach a point where exercise isn't viewed as compensation for food or a form of punishment.

Wear Clothes That Fit

Have you ever bought clothes that are too small, hoping they'd motivate you to lose weight? When you find yourself still unable to wear them weeks or months later, it triggers self-criticism, self-loathing and annoyance at oneself for having failed again. I admit to engaging in this behaviour for years, and unfortunately, it only intensified my negative body image and self-talk, creating a detrimental cycle.

Many of us squeeze into clothes that are too small because we aspire to be that size and feel ashamed that we are a size bigger than we want to be. This approach leads to feelings of extreme self-consciousness and unbearable discomfort throughout the day. When working on improving body image it is fundamental to prioritize wearing clothes that fit and ones that make you feel comfortable.

In our society, there is an all-encompassing stigma attached to clothing sizes, wherein anything beyond a UK size 10 (US size 12) can make you feel that you are too large. Conversely, smaller sizes are often glorified as remarkable achievements. It's crucial to remind ourselves that clothing sizes are merely numbers, and different stores have varying measurement standards. It's truly outrageous to gauge our worth based on these arbitrary numbers.

Why not take a stand against this mindset? You could start by eliminating all the clothes that make you feel terrible about yourself and instead embrace clothes that fit you and make you feel comfortable. When shopping, prioritize buying clothes that truly match your body shape and size and shift your focus to self-acceptance and personal comfort.

Be Around Those Who Are Supportive

Do you sit and cringe when people bond over diet chat, the size of their bodies and, worst of all, other people's bodies?

When working on improving your body image it is vital to examine what people you are mostly around and what attitudes they have about food and bodies. I fully comprehend the difficulty of finding individuals who are on the same page. I know first-hand that being around family members who are fixated on food, weight and body size can be a particularly challenging and triggering situation. Setting boundaries is crucial.

Here are a few suggestions for dealing with weight and size obsessed individuals:

- Completely change the subject to something like, "Oh where are you going on holiday?"
- Say, "I don't really find it that interesting talking about other people's body sizes. I am done with dieting."
- Walk away.

Ensuring your own wellbeing requires establishing robust boundaries. It might be time for you to proactively confront individuals, limit your interactions with them, or even consider cutting them out of your life entirely. Taking steps to distance yourself and set boundaries with those who negatively impact your body image can help immensely.

Be Aware of All Your Triggers

It is essential to have a comprehensive understanding of all your triggers. It might be helpful to compile a list of factors that evoke negative feelings about your body, empowering you to promptly acknowledge, confront and fathom what it is that exacerbates these emotions and behaviours related to your body.

Allow me to share a compilation of factors that once triggered me, with the hope that it will aid you in identifying your own triggers and fostering a deeper understanding of what influences you:

Dieting, exposure to media images, mirror checking, seeing my reflection, weighing myself, being around certain people, exposure to trashy magazines, eating certain foods, comments from others, comparing my body to others, being alone, feeling overwhelmed or bored or angry, feeling let down or misunderstood or powerless or ignored or invalidated or gaslighted, not achieving the high standard that I set myself.

Only when you identify your own triggers will you be able to set healthy boundaries. Being self-aware is fundamental on the journey to improved body image.

Feel Your Emotions

At times, experiencing negative emotions about one's body has little to do with how it appears physically. Fixating on body size becomes a distracting deception. In truth, something much deeper lies beneath the surface. For many individuals – including myself – a significant aspect of overcoming negative body image entails reconnecting with your authentic self and confronting suppressed and painful emotions that have resided within since childhood.

When you were little were you ever on the receiving end of any of the following comments?

- "Cheer up for goodness' sake!"
- "What have you got to be sad about?"
- "Stop making a fuss!"
- "I'll give you something to cry about."

- "There's no need to be angry."
- "Just keep your mouth shut."
- "Stop crying." (in Scotland, "Stop greetin.")
- "Nobody asked your opinion."

When an individual's childhood is marked by an inability to freely express emotions, alternative channels of expression often emerge, frequently manifesting as self-criticism toward the body. Engaging in therapy to confront childhood trauma can be instrumental in fostering healing and positively transforming one's body image.

Steps On Your Journey

As this chapter comes to its conclusion the journey toward improving body image encompasses a range of essential steps. At its heart is the cultivation of self-compassion and self-care. It also involves:

- Challenging negative thoughts and aligning behaviours with a healthier body image.
- Examining and challenging societal expectations, understanding triggers and rejecting harmful influences.
- Letting go of perfectionism, embracing uniqueness and practicing self-acceptance.
- Replacing unhealthy habits with ones that prioritize comfort and wellbeing and curating a positive environment both online and in real life.
- Allowing yourself to process emotions, reinforcing positivity through affirmations, and celebrating your qualities and accomplishments.
- Engaging in activities that foster self-connection and staying true to your values.
- Educating yourself, cultivating gratitude, and remembering to be patient with yourself when on this journey.

- Seeking professional support may help you as you progress toward a healthier body image.

To sum up, prioritizing the improvement of body image will not only benefit *you* it will also contribute to breaking the cycle of body image issues in children. When we treat ourselves with kindness, our children learn important lessons. When we educate ourselves, we educate our children. Understanding and rejecting harmful societal influences helps us to create a positive environment that nurtures body acceptance and leads to a happier more peaceful life for the whole family.

When we foster healthy relationships with our bodies, celebrate their uniqueness and appreciate how they function we teach children that they are more than a body. By modelling self-care, body acceptance and body positivity, we empower the younger generation. We help to create a generation of individuals who prioritize wellbeing and cultivate a positive body image that lasts a lifetime. As we continue to challenge deeply ingrained beliefs and societal messaging, we are making progress for the next generation.

7

THE ESSENTIALS OF
POSITIVE ROLE MODELLING

The adults in a child's life hold significant influence over how they develop their attitudes toward food and their bodies. The number one way our children learn is through social modelling – observing the adults around them. Within the walls of our homes, we have the power to shape our children's perceptions, instilling in them the values of self-acceptance, positive body image and a healthy attitude toward food. By actively engaging in the process of unlearning harmful societal norms, we can disrupt the cycle and pave the way for a healthier, more empowered generation.

This chapter explores the crucial role parents play as agents of positive role modelling, highlighting how our actions, words and attitudes toward food and body image can profoundly influence our children's wellbeing. By harnessing this power, we can guide them on a journey of self-love, build resilience and instil in them a lifelong commitment to their own physical and emotional health. The encouraging news is that your children don't have to inherit any body image insecurities or concerns over food that you have, ones that have been deeply ingrained over generations. You can learn to be a positive role model for them, regardless of what stage you are at on your own journey to food and body freedom.

As was discussed in depth in chapter 2 we learned that there are multiple ways in which we unknowingly impact our children's relationships with food and their bodies. Recognizing these influences is crucial, and this chapter is dedicated to enhancing that awareness. While external factors like social media, advertising and the impact of peers wield considerable, uncontrollable sway, there are several elements under our control that we can proactively address. In the upcoming sections, we will delve into a variety of strategies to successfully achieve this objective.

To cultivate positive attitudes toward food, weight, shape and body image in children, it is essential that the adults in their lives convey more appropriate messages to them. As role models it is fundamental to begin by addressing the behaviours and the language used in their presence. Children observe our actions, listen to our conversations and absorb the language we employ. When adults are engaging in chat that includes criticism of body size, weight concerns and body shape complaints, it is easy to assume that children are not paying attention. However, these discussions can significantly contribute to their own dissatisfaction with their bodies.

Let's explore how we can serve as positive role models for our children.

Stop Commenting On Bodies

Refraining from commenting on your own body, your child's body, or anyone's body while in the presence of children is of paramount importance. When it comes to the appearance of bodies, silence is the best approach. If you think a body looks fantastic, say nothing. Likewise, if you consider a body to be horrible or ugly, also say nothing.

Multiple research studies underscore the detrimental effects of commenting on bodies in any context while in the presence of children, showing that these conversations contribute to the development of negative body image and self-esteem issues that often last a lifetime.

As you'll now be aware, I was raised in a family where discussing bodies was commonplace, with frequent conversations about an individual's weight fluctuations or body size. This upbringing instilled in me the belief that body size held great importance, fostering a heightened sense of self-consciousness about my own weight and size.

Stop Idolizing Thin Bodies

"The best-known environmental contributor to the development of eating disorders is the sociocultural idealization of thinness."[24]

Idolizing thin bodies is commonplace in our society and doing so in front of children can be dangerous for several reasons. Firstly, it promotes unrealistic beauty standards, which can lead to body dissatisfaction and low self-esteem in children who don't fit into those narrow ideals. This can contribute to the development of eating disorders such as bulimia nervosa, binge eating disorder and anorexia nervosa, as children strive to attain these unrealistic standards. Additionally, it can perpetuate the harmful notion that one's worth is tied to their appearance, rather than their character, talents or actions. Worshipping thin bodies in front of children also neglects the diversity of body types and sizes, reinforcing harmful stereotypes and fostering a culture of body shaming and discrimination. Instead, it's crucial to promote body positivity and acceptance, teaching children to value themselves and others for who they are rather than how they look.

End the Diet Conversation

Anyone who has engaged in dieting will tell you that what you restrict is what you will obsess over. It leads to an unhealthy fixation on food and body shape, often resulting in lifelong body insecurities, low self-esteem and an increased likelihood of developing an eating disorder. It is crucial to be aware of the dangers of dieting and to refrain from engaging in or discussing them in front of children. Many individuals who suffer from an eating disorder will tell you that it all started with a diet.

Don't even mention the word "diet" until your child is old enough to understand (and analyse) diet culture. Avoid any weight related conversations if they are within earshot. If you are secretly on a diet, trying to lose a few pounds, keep it a secret. Shield your child. They do not need to know about scales or calories or measurements or anything at all to do with diets. As they grow older and become more aware of diet culture, have open and candid conversations with them about it.

When we diet in front of children, we teach them that only a small body is acceptable. We teach them that healthy equals thin. We teach them that restricting is normal. We teach them that exercise is a chore. We teach them not to love or accept themselves. By stopping dieting, we teach our children to trust their bodies natural cues, to honour its wants and needs and to have a peaceful relationship with food and their body size.

I spent my childhood observing my elders on diets and through my extensive involvement in eating disorder support groups, I encountered numerous individuals who also traced their early exposure to parental dieting as a major influence in their pursuit of a thin body and subsequent struggles. Studies consistently indicate that children who witness dieting behaviours are more likely to engage in dieting themselves and those who diet are eight times more likely to develop an eating disorder.

Never Ever Put Your Child On a Diet!

It is critical to refrain from ever putting your child on a diet. Such a decision could result in lifelong challenges related to food and body image. It has the capacity to significantly harm their life, causing them to feel unaccepted, unloved and fundamentally flawed. It can lead to secret eating, binge eating, engaging in harmful weight loss strategies and (the opposite of the desired effect) weight gain.

Ginny Jones, an expert in this field, aptly states in one of her Instagram posts:

"If you are encouraging your child to avoid weight gain, you are inviting an eating disorder into your house."[25]

Instead, let us embrace the notion of unconditional love for our children, irrespective of their size or shape. The size of their body should never be a factor or topic of discussion. Let us cherish our children for who they are as individuals, wholly separate from their appearance.

Stop Comparing Body Sizes

It is of paramount importance to avoid comparing your child's body to that of others. This practice carries profound significance. Such comparisons only serve to emphasize to children that their size is a matter of concern.

In my years of working in support groups, many individuals vividly recalled experiences where their body size was compared with that of siblings or friends. In many cases it led to heightened self-consciousness and reinforced to them that their body size was under scrutiny.

Instead, let's promote body acceptance and refrain from actions or statements that imply any inherent flaws in their bodies. Embrace the fact that some children may be smaller or larger for their age, even if they are twins; some may be skinny, while others might be fat. Every child is equally valuable, and it's important to bear in mind that discussing these matters can be potentially harmful.

Stop Fussing Over Food

Equally important is to avoid unnecessary emphasis on food. Refrain from making comments regarding food choices, your own food choices, or the choices of others. It should come as no surprise that when we excessively focus on food, children are more likely to develop food-related problems as they grow older. When we avoid the creation of a food and weight-centric environment, we help prevent issues from arising.

Refrain from commenting on the quantity a child consumes. Many parents engage in food shaming with good intentions, unaware of the negative effects it can have on a child's relationship with food. Food shaming can be toxic, leading to behaviours such as secretive eating, binge eating, emotional eating or restrictive eating.

Comments such as, "How can someone so little eat all that?" or "You better not eat all that!" can profoundly impact a child's perception of themselves and their relationship with food. Let us learn that by not magnifying the issue, we can prevent it from becoming one. The best course of action is, of course, to say nothing at all.

Numerous individuals have recounted how comments about what they ate made them feel ashamed or labelled them as greedy. Some were even denied certain foods, which caused them to develop strong cravings or engage in binge eating. Additionally, using food as a reward can create an unhealthy pattern of seeking comfort through eating.

If there is a genuine need to discuss food, it may be helpful to educate children about its function in the body and emphasize that it serves not only as fuel but also as a source of pleasure in life. Mealtimes should be approached with a relaxed and enjoyable atmosphere, where children feel comfortable expressing their preferences. Children possess an innate sense of what they like or dislike; when they are hungry and when they are full. Trusting their instincts in these matters is vital.

Stop Labelling Food

A child's first taste of disordered eating is when foods are restricted at home and are called "bad". Avoid labelling food in front of children. Food does not possess moral value: it is neither inherently good nor bad. When we categorize certain foods as bad, such as sweets or biscuits, and deny them to our children, it can result in them developing a sense of shame around these specific foods, especially if they like them. This can often lead to cravings and secretive eating behaviours as they seek out what has been restricted or forbidden.

It is important to create an environment where all foods are allowed and accepted within the home. By removing the labels and restrictions, we can foster a healthy relationship with food and prevent the onset of problematic behaviours.

Get Rid of the Scales

Having bathroom scales at home can be dangerous, especially in terms of influencing body image and creating a connection with weight and body size. These seemingly innocent devices can unknowingly contribute to the development of a negative self-perception and an unhealthy fixation on a number. When scales are readily accessible, they send a message to children that worth is determined by a number, overshadowing the importance of our overall health, happiness and qualities as a person. This can foster a preoccupation with a number, leading to body dissatisfaction, low self-esteem and potentially even the development of disordered eating habits.

Removing bathroom scales from our homes helps to free ourselves from the constraints of arbitrary measurements and to embrace a more compassionate relationship with our bodies. We are more than a number and our children are more than a number. Scales merely provide information on your relationship with gravity; they say nothing about your worth as an individual.

So why not get rid of your bathroom scales? Stop being a slave to a scale. Our children do not need to know about scales or their weight.

Never *Ever* Weigh Your Child

This is crucial. Individuals who suffer from eating disorders often recall the distressing experiences of being weighed as a child. This action almost always results in intense feelings of shame and embarrassment, particularly if the child's weight is compared to that of their peers. Weighing children not only highlights their size but can also trigger a harmful desire to change their bodies. This, in turn, could trigger the adoption of dangerous weight loss behaviours, such as obsessive exercise or disordered eating patterns.

Keep Unhealthy Media Out of Sight

Leaving "trashy" magazines lying around the house can often teach children a dangerous message even if they can't read. Front cover content predominantly revolves around appearance, body sizes, weights and diets, often promoting "body transformations" or giving tips on how to achieve the "perfect beach body". It teaches children that this is what is important – the size of their body. Consider the lessons these magazines may be imparting to your child.

As a child, I absorbed information about diets, weights, measurements and body sizes from flipping through my mum's magazines that were left on the kitchen table or on the living room floor. They always applauded weight loss and stigmatized weight gain, subjecting women's bodies to severe scrutiny and criticism. The message in the magazines only reinforced what I already believed.

Be Aware of Discussion About Clothing Choices

Making comments around little ones such as, "I've got nothing to wear", when you have a cupboard full of options, conveys a message to a child that there is something wrong with your body. Children have sharp observation skills; they see the abundance of clothes you have and can decipher the underlying meaning behind such statements.

Let's shift the perspective and teach children that we feel gratitude for the abundance of clothes we have and for the diversity of styles and colours available to us. This way, we can impart a positive message, emphasizing that our clothing allows us to showcase our personality and creativity, and the most important thing is how our clothes make us *feel*, not how our body looks.

Teach Children to Appreciate Their Bodies

Teaching children to appreciate and be proud of every single little part of their bodies is a vital part of teaching body acceptance. Educating them on the physical wonders of their body can be a fun thing to do and in turn help us on our own journey of self-healing and body acceptance.

Make a habit of talking about how grateful you are for your strong body, highlighting, for example, that strong legs allow you to run and jump and hop and skip. Draw attention to what specific parts of the body allow us to do and why you are grateful for that. Showing appreciation for what bodies can do over how they look will be hugely beneficial for your children.

Embrace Body Diversity

We can effortlessly cultivate a home environment where every body type is celebrated and appreciated. We can engage in discussions about the diversity of bodies, fostering a non-judgmental attitude toward those that may not conform to societal standards. It's crucial for our children to understand and embrace the uniqueness of all bodies.

When adults laugh at or body shame individuals due to their size, children pick up on these harmful attitudes. By doing so, children learn to mock or scrutinize those who may be perceived as "too fat", "too big", "too skinny", or "too tall", making such comments seem acceptable. Of course, children will naturally make comparisons and discuss others' physical appearances, however it is our responsibility to underscore that every body, regardless of its shape or size, deserves love and respect.

As a kid, I internalized messages that only one body type – specifically a thin one – was considered worthy. My elders, who continually made negative remarks about fat bodies, created a home environment where body shaming was the norm and only thin bodies were deemed acceptable.

It is our responsibility to engage in open, positive and loving conversations about all body types. Ask your children how they feel when they see girls in sticker books or movies or on shows who all look the same. Ask them if they think it is possible to be successful and happy if they don't look like them. We can emphasize to children that no two bodies are alike, and that every one of them adds richness and intrigue to life. We want them to be aware that it is safe to exist in any body, that it doesn't have to fit a narrow ideal to be worthy of love and respect.

Warn of the Dangers of Teasing

As children become increasingly conscious of their own physical appearances and begin comparing themselves to peers they will naturally engage in body-related comments and tease one another. They will notice differences in size or features, like someone having a larger body or a distinctive nose.

Our role as adults is to instil the understanding that every individual's physical body is unique, and one is not superior to another. It is crucial to emphasize that it's not acceptable to mock or make fun of someone's appearance; while explaining the emotional harm it can inflict. Encourage them to stand up and speak out against such behaviour at school.

Many individuals who have experienced eating disorders can trace the origins of their body insecurities back to teasing and bullying related to their appearance.

Focus On a Person's Qualities

Placing less emphasis on a person's appearance and more on their personality and other meaningful facets of their life is a powerful way to instil belief in a child that we are all more than a body. It is well within our power to shift attention away from physical appearance entirely and foster positive conversations about ourselves and others, emphasizing qualities, values and strengths.

Encourage conversations that revolve around aspects unrelated to physical looks and more centred on a person's character and virtues. Enquire why they appreciate individuals – for instance, the neighbour next door because she's always friendly and upbeat, or their teacher who may be funny, or their grandad who is kind and full of fun. Prompt them to identify the qualities and attributes they admire in people. This helps children understand that a person's worth is based on their actions rather than their physical appearance.

Such education empowers children to develop empathy and respect for others, as they recognize that every individual is different, and each have their own special qualities and strengths.

Celebrate Inherent Qualities

Encourage children to recognize their own strengths and qualities and to celebrate their successes and achievements. Highlight their strengths: make them feel special by praising their football, skipping or drawing skills, how well they ride a bike or how good they are at singing or doing handstands. Take an interest in what are they reading, what they love to play with, to watch on TV, or to listen to. Chat to them about it even if it doesn't interest you in the slightest. Taking an interest in their life is such a massive part of helping your child to feel secure within themselves which in turn helps to build self-worth and self-esteem.

Always make them feel like they are an important member of the family and that they have valuable contributions. Highlight what they do for others and praise them for being kind or thoughtful or for being a good brother or sister. Vocalize how impressed you are when you see them getting along well with others and compliment them when they do something kind, caring or thoughtful.

Do the same for others in front of your children. Compliment what someone is good at and what qualities you admire in them as a person, their bravery, their tenacity, their hard work ethic, their calming personality, their ability to forgive. Focussing on the qualities of a person rather than their appearance helps children to see that we are more than a body. It will do wonders for their self-confidence.

This quote by Brooke Hampton truly resonates: "Speak to your children as if they are the wisest, kindest, most beautiful and magical humans on earth, for what they believe is what they will become!"[26]

Focus On Body Function

Teaching children about the marvels of how the human body functions, as opposed to emphasising its appearance, offers a multitude of invaluable benefits. Firstly, it fosters a deep sense of appreciation and gratitude for the body's capabilities. By understanding how their bodies work, children can develop a profound connection with their physical selves and become more attuned to the incredible things it can do. This knowledge encourages a positive and healthy body image as it shifts the focus away from societal beauty ideals and toward a genuine understanding of the remarkable abilities of the human body such as strength, flexibility, resilience and adaptability.

Allow Children to Express Emotions

Creating an emotion-friendly household where children can openly express themselves is a profoundly beneficial approach for nurturing their emotional and psychological wellbeing. Firstly, it fosters strong parent–child relationships built on trust and understanding. When children feel free to share their thoughts and emotions, it promotes open communication and a sense of security, knowing that their feelings are valued. This, in turn, equips children with essential emotional intelligence, helping them identify, manage and express their emotions in a healthy manner. Moreover, an emotion-friendly home environment teaches children empathy and compassion, as they learn to appreciate and respect the emotions of others. It also reduces the likelihood of emotional repression, which can lead to behavioural issues or mental health challenges in the future.

Many eating disorder sufferers disclose that their emotions were invalidated as children, which led them to express themselves through food and their body. Being on the receiving end of comments like, "I will give you something to cry for" or "What have you got to cry about?" when emotions were expressed made it unsafe to show real emotions and led to a deep distrust of oneself.

A household that encourages emotional expression empowers children to develop into well-adjusted, confident individuals who can form strong, positive relationships both within and outside the family.

Encourage a Healthy and Active Lifestyle

Fostering an active family lifestyle offers a plethora of benefits, particularly in terms of enhancing the body image of children. When a family engages in regular physical activities together, it promotes a positive association with exercise and a healthy relationship with their bodies. Children learn to appreciate their bodies for what they can do, rather than how they look. This perspective shift emphasizes functionality and wellbeing over appearance, which can greatly boost self-esteem. Additionally, active family time provides an opportunity for parents to model and instil healthy habits, setting the foundation for a lifetime of physical wellness. Exercising together also strengthens family bonds, creating a supportive environment where children feel secure and loved, reducing the likelihood of body image issues stemming from insecurities. Overall, an active family lifestyle not only fosters physical health but also promotes a strong and positive body image, setting children on a path to self-confidence and a healthy relationship with their bodies.

Challenge Media Messaging

Teaching media literacy to children is a powerful tool for equipping them with the skills and awareness to navigate a world rife with diet culture messaging. By understanding the tactics and strategies employed by media outlets to promote unrealistic beauty ideals and weight-loss fads, we can teach children to develop a critical eye. This will enable them to decipher between manipulated images and reality, reducing the potential for body image dissatisfaction and unrealistic standards.

Moreover, media literacy empowers children to make informed and conscious choices about the content they consume, promoting a sense of autonomy and self-esteem. It encourages a questioning mindset, fostering the ability to challenge harmful diet culture narratives and advocate for a more balanced and healthy approach to self-image. In essence, teaching media literacy not only protects children from the negative impact of diet culture messaging but also equips them with the tools to become resilient, self-aware individuals who can resist the pressures of unrealistic beauty ideals. The next chapter provides a more comprehensive exploration of this topic.

Protect Children From Weight-Related Comments

We must actively shield our children from individuals who make disparaging remarks about appearances or engage in teasing. Setting boundaries with family and friends is crucial. When conversations take a concerning turn into the realm of body size, diets and weight-related worries, it's essential to confront such discussions in the presence of children. Be prepared to challenge it or have a polite reason to disengage. If older children are present, take the opportunity to explain to them why you chose to change the subject or remove yourself from the conversation. By doing so, we create a protective barrier against the harmful impact of negative body image discussions, promoting a healthier and more positive environment for children to thrive.

Discuss Puberty

Adolescence can prove to be a challenging time characterized by rapid and often unwelcome changes in the body. Engaging in open conversations with children is a beneficial and essential practice for various reasons. Firstly, it provides them with accurate information and knowledge, dispelling myths and misconceptions that may otherwise cause anxiety or confusion. By understanding the natural changes that occur during puberty, children are better prepared to navigate this transformative phase in their lives. These discussions foster a sense of comfort and an acceptance of their changing bodies, reducing potential insecurities and self-esteem issues.

Adolescents will naturally place significance on their physical appearance, the opinions of others, and making comparisons. It's normal for them to take numerous selfies, striving to look their best, and seeking acceptance. We should avoid shaming them for these behaviours or for spending time in front of the mirror experimenting with makeup and fashion. Instead, strive to be a source of support and empathy, understanding the unique challenges they face in a world that exposes them to more than we ever experienced in our own youth. They need to feel heard and acknowledged during these transformative years.

Furthermore, open communication about puberty promotes a healthier body image, as children learn to embrace and appreciate their bodies as they evolve. It also encourages a trusting and supportive parent–child relationship, as children feel they can turn to their caregivers for guidance and reassurance. Ultimately, these conversations contribute to emotional wellbeing and overall self-confidence, allowing children to face the challenges of puberty with greater resilience and understanding.

Focus On What We Can Do

As we draw this chapter to a close, we are hopefully more aware of the profound influence we hold as role models in our children's lives and of how we can transform this destructive pattern that runs through families. We have no control over the external pressures and noise from the outside world. What we can do is shape and control the dynamics within our homes. Offering a solid foundation gives our children an added layer of protection against the diet culture and beauty industry giants, who will undoubtedly get their claws into them somewhere along the road. We can take it upon ourselves to play an active role in preventing the next generation from developing negative body images and disordered relationships with food.

To effect this change let us reflect on the key insights taken from the chapter.

- We must acknowledge that our actions, our words, and even our subtlest behaviours can leave a lasting impact on our children's relationship with food and their bodies. Children closely observe our attitudes toward eating, exercise and self-image.
- Let's put an end to the comparisons, dieting, judgments and the idolization of specific body types. Let's end the cycle of fussing over food, body shaming and calorie counting. Instead, let's aim to impart the profound understanding that every body – irrespective of its shape or size – is an extraordinary organism.
- We must instil in children the values of tolerance and non-judgment toward bodies that do not fit society's narrow definition of "perfection".
- We must shift our focus toward the qualities, personalities and achievements of individuals, valuing them for who they are rather than how they look.

- We must show genuine interest in children's interests, thoughts, feelings and emotions, and cultivate the belief in children that they are more than just their physical body.
- We can educate and shield our children, strengthen their resilience, and significantly influence how they perceive their bodies and their relationship with food as they mature.

To reshape the narrative around body image would be nothing short of revolutionary. The time for change must be now, and it begins within our homes.

8

NURTURING MEDIA LITERACY FOR OUR CHILDREN'S WELLBEING

In today's complex and interconnected world, where screens and media surround us, the need for media literacy has never been more critical. Exposure to an overload of information via different technologies plays a central role in all our lives. It is pivotal that we develop a set of skills that enables us to critically analyse media messages, including the identification of biases, propaganda and misinformation. It is crucial that we evaluate information sources for credibility and develop the ability to distinguish between fact and opinion.

Our children are extremely vulnerable to media pressure because they lack experience and the emotional maturity to understand, filter or moderate the messages they are exposed to. This chapter explores the paramount importance of cultivating media literacy in our children, with a particular focus on how it safeguards their emotional wellbeing and resilience in the face of pervasive messages surrounding body image, diets and digitally enhanced images. It delves into the pivotal role parents and caregivers play in being better role models, advocating for safe and limited media use, understanding how media impacts our and our children's emotions and behaviours, and how we can cultivate a better relationship with it.

Children today find themselves immersed in a torrent of media from various sources. A computer is the possession most children couldn't live without. Video game advertisements, internet memes shared through phone messages, and an array of social media platforms including YouTube, Instagram, Snapchat, Facebook, TikTok and X (formally Twitter) expose them to an overwhelming volume of messages daily. They are also confronted with traditional media, such as TV, radio, newspapers and magazines. Even very young children absorb messages from sources like TV advertisements, toys, cartoons and movies, often unaware of the subliminal messaging.

Children receive mobile phones at increasingly young ages, exposing them to the pressures of social media before they've fully discovered their true selves. They face immense pressure to conform to idealized standards of appearance and to constantly seek validation in the critical world of social media. The prevalence of reality TV shows exacerbates the phenomenon that they must have the "perfect body", causing young individuals to subject themselves to harsh self-assessment. Consequently, one's physical appearance becomes a yardstick for measuring self-worth, and any perceived imperfections can lead to profound discontent and, ultimately, anxiety, depression and problems with body image.

The annual research carried out by Girlguiding UK reveals how girls feels about the appearance pressures that they face. The charity's 15th annual Girls' Attitudes Survey, conducted in 2023, showed some worrying finds:

- In 2009, 72% of girls aged 7–21 said they are happy with how they looked. This has fallen to 59% in 2023.
- 68% of girls aged 11–21 have said they'd like to lose weight and half have been on a diet (53%) or skipped a meal to lose weight (48%).
- A third of girls said they would consider plastic surgery, which has risen over the last 5 years (34% in 2023 compared to 29% in 2018).

- 62% of girls and young women aged 7–21 report being criticized or have had mean things said about how they look, compared to 49% in 2016.
- Over two-thirds of girls (67%) say they sometimes feel ashamed of the way they look because they're not like girls and women they see in the media and online.
- 39% of girls aged 11–21 state that seeing images online where people are edited to look perfect makes them feel bad about they look and feel.[27]

These results are devastating and highlight the increasing pressures our girls face. To contemplate that a child's self-esteem these days is closely tied to the number of likes they receive, how many followers they have, or how they are rated by their peers is terrifying.

A friend of mine recently revealed that their daughter discovered she had been rated "2 out of 10" for her looks by boys in her school year. She felt a deep sense of shame and embarrassment, reaching the point of not wanting to return to school. It's genuinely alarming to contemplate the profound impact a single instance of body criticism can have on a child's mental health.

In less-industrialized societies of the past, children were not exposed to the overwhelming abundance of images as they are today. Although, personally, coming of age in an era without the internet, I believe my perspectives were significantly shaped by the images I encountered, undoubtedly harming my self-esteem and body image. I felt tremendous pressure to imitate what I was exposed to in the 1990s. What I can't even begin to fathom is the impact it would have had on my mental wellbeing if I had been subjected to the volume of messages that today's youth are confronted with. It is unprecedented.

Where do we begin in addressing this modern-day problem? Let's attempt to dissect it into smaller, more manageable sections. The subsequent list suggests several recommendations for developing media literacy as a family, which we will unpack in more depth in this chapter.

- Understand what media literacy is and why it's important
- Consider how we as adults use the media and how we are affected by it
- Our role as positive role models – setting boundaries and safe use
- Develop our children's ability to critically analyse advertisements and media messages
- Foster an awareness within our children of digital manipulation and its impact on body image
- Encourage open discussions about body diversity and the danger of internalizing unrealistic ideals

What Is Media Literacy and Why Is It Crucial?

Media literacy is being able to analyse and interpret messages conveyed through various media formats. It refers to the ability to access, analyse, evaluate and create media in various forms, such as print, digital, audio or visual content. It involves developing a set of skills and critical thinking abilities that enable individuals to navigate the complex and ever-evolving media landscape safely and effectively.

Media literacy empowers individuals to interpret the messages they encounter, to question assumptions, and to make informed decisions about the media consumed and produced. In simple terms, media literacy gives people the skills to think carefully about media, helping them become more informed.

Media literacy within families is crucial when it comes to educating children against the pervasive influence of diet culture. It empowers children to be able to critically analyse media messages, decipher unrealistic ideals perpetuated by the fashion and beauty industries, and cultivate a resilient sense of self-worth. By fostering media literacy, families provide the tools necessary for children to resist harmful messages surrounding body image, diets and societal pressures, ultimately promoting a healthier and more empowered relationship with media content.

Recognizing the Influence of Media On Our Lives

One of the initial steps in addressing the media's impact on our children is to acknowledge the significant influence it wields in our own lives. As adults, we are constantly plugged into our phones, incessantly messaging and monitoring social media platforms such as Facebook, Instagram and TikTok. We often feel overwhelmed by the pressure to keep pace with this fast-paced digital environment.

Taking the time to reflect and monitor our screentime is crucial. It's important to grasp how the images and messages we encounter influence our emotions and behaviours. You may find it beneficial to keep a record over the next few days: note the duration of time spent on each platform and pay attention to any advertisements, pop-ups or suggested content you come across on television or your laptop, as well as on your social media feeds.

To help you better understand the impact of the media in your own life it might be helpful to reflect upon the following:

- Consider the underlying messages and intentions of the content you encounter.
- Reflect on the emotional impact they have on you.
- Assess whether they exert a positive or negative influence.
- Explore how images, advertisements and messages shape your self-image.
- Contemplate the emotions evoked when confronted with the glorification of weight loss on platforms like Instagram or in magazines.

- Examine how exposure to specific measurements and weights of your favourite actors affects your self-perception.
- Analyse your thoughts when encountering advertisements promising a "Perfect beach body in 10 days" or a complete body transformation.
- Evaluate your emotional response to ads for procedures like weight loss surgery, Botox, tanning, breast enlargement, eyebrow enhancement or eyelash extensions.

With regards to diet culture and the beauty industry, every message we are exposed to promotes a singular theme: the need to change your appearance. These adverts insinuate that by following certain actions, you can enhance your appearance. It's important to acknowledge that this form of media functions as a powerful means of mass communication, primarily aiming to capture our attention and, in turn, shape our thoughts and behaviours.

Exposure to digitally altered images and relentless diet culture messaging can lead to feelings of inadequacy, low self-esteem, anxiety and depression – and to body dissatisfaction and eating disorders. The emotional and behavioural repercussions of these messages can be significant. Consider the immense influence they wield over vulnerable children and young teenagers who may lack the emotional maturity to comprehend their implications.

The Role of Parents and Caregivers As Role Models

As parents and caregivers, we are the primary guides in teaching children how to navigate the digital world safely, critically, and confidently. We can create a supportive environment where children feel safe discussing media content and its impact on their lives. Children are avid observers, closely monitoring the behaviours and attitudes of the adults in their lives. To foster media literacy, parents and caregivers must serve as exemplary role models. This means not only encouraging responsible media use but also demonstrating a healthy relationship with media content.

Here are some ways parents and caregivers can play an active role:

Open and Honest Dialogue

Encourage open and honest conversations about the media. Create a space where children can express their thoughts and feelings about the content they encounter without fear of judgment. It's important to empathize with what is important to them – the times they are living through is an era that is alien to us. For example, posting selfies to gather likes is possibly what matters most to them; however, encourage them to see that they are more than a photo on a social media platform.

When children feel listened to, they are more inclined to seek guidance and confide their concerns. By fostering direct and sincere communication with our children, we provide them with the opportunity to comprehend our perspectives and apprehensions. You may find they initially dismiss these viewpoints in favour of following the latest trends, perceiving it as excessive interference or nagging or trying to spoil their fun. The key here lies in exercising patience. While they may not immediately grasp the truth, it is worthwhile to instil awareness and establish a sturdy foundation to shield them from the influence of aggressive media. This additional layer of protection aids in enhancing their awareness and resilience against pervasive, insidious messages. As they mature, they may come to appreciate that our intentions were always geared toward safeguarding their wellbeing.

Set Screentime Boundaries

Establish reasonable limits on screentime and device usage. Create a media use schedule that allows for a balance between online and offline activities. Consistency is key, and parents should lead by example by adhering to these boundaries themselves. If your child observes you frequently engrossed in your phone or absorbed in your computer, you are inadvertently communicating that such behaviour is acceptable. Establishing reasonable limits on screentime benefits everyone. Striking a balance between digital and offline activities is pivotal in nurturing a child's wellbeing and development.

Make Sure Children Are Safe Online

To protect our children from harmful content it's important to monitor your child's online activities and to enforce parental controls on electronic devices. Without being overly controlling, utilizing parental controls available on both televisions and computers is one effective method to regulate their exposure. These controls can even block specific keywords.

Groomers and hackers target the most vulnerable: our children. It's a terrifying thought that one of the most dangerous places a child can be in today's era is on their own in their bedroom with a phone or a computer. The hacking of content intended for children serves as a stark reminder of the need to diligently monitor the content your child consumes to ensure their safety and wellbeing.

As children grow older, understanding the online landscape your child navigates is crucial. Be aware of their interests and what matters to them. Ensuring the websites and video games they access are age-appropriate is essential, given the frequent appearance of unsolicited pop-up ads.

Despite actively blocking every diet ad or weight loss programme, I still encounter pop-ups on my feed trying to lure me into body transformation programmes.

Be aware of pro-anorexia (pro-ana) websites which are typically characterized by their focus on thinness and weight loss. They often provide tips on how to restrict food intake, purge and exercise excessively. These websites may also contain images of dangerously thin individuals and promote the idea that thinness is the only way to be attractive and successful. Although social media companies and eating disorder organizations have taken steps to combat pro-anorexia websites and Instagram accounts, they are still a serious concern. These accounts often normalize and glorify harmful behaviours and can be particularly detrimental to young people.

We must implement robust measures to help ensure that our children do not readily come across dangerous or age-inappropriate content on digital platforms.

Teach Critical Thinking

Media literacy involves the role of actively teaching children critical thinking skills, helping them to recognize the difference between fact and opinion, assess the credibility of information sources, and understand the persuasive techniques employed by media.

The latest diet or exercise trend are almost always accompanied by images of impeccably sculpted and artificially "enhanced" models. Our young girls are unaware that many of these depictions aren't even real. This "fake" image of perfection becomes embedded into their subconscious. While their ideas about themselves, their bodies, their place in society are forming and developing they are sold the idea that they must look like the perfect woman: tall, tanned, thin but curvy, flawless skin, long legs, no cellulite, accentuated lips, shiny hair, perfectly proportioned breasts.

It might be helpful to engage with your child to look for real-life examples that illustrate the perfect image. The aim is to get children to question what they are seeing instead of being subjected to it without understanding what it means.

A worthwhile and fun activity to engage with your child might include looking out for different messages on TV, on social media, in magazines and on websites that suggest they should alter their bodies or promote diets and weight loss. Initiate open discussions about the messages conveyed, prompting them to identify if the ads are promoting a product or encouraging specific activities. This encourages them to ponder the source's intent: Who created it, and for what purpose? Is the message authentic? Do the images depict reality? Are the messages truthful? Most importantly, they learn to gauge how these media portrayals affect their self-perception. In doing so, they develop an awareness of the underlying motives and beneficiaries behind certain behaviours and thoughts, arming them with the resilience to steer clear of the pitfalls we've encountered. Feel free to share personal experiences, recounting how similar advertisements affected you and made you feel inadequate, leading to efforts to conform through product purchases, diet attempts and strenuous exercise routines.

This exercise offers valuable insights into the subtle-yet-pervasive nature of diet culture and its purpose, helping children understand how the media communicates with us and how it tries to influence our thoughts and our behaviours. Diet culture's fundamental goal is to instil a sense of inadequacy, pressuring individuals to transform their bodies to meet unrealistic ideals. While we may not have complete control over everything our children encounter or the extent of its influence, we can certainly raise their awareness regarding the role of the media and its potential impact on their lives.

Discuss Digital Manipulation

It is crucial to introduce children to the concept of digital manipulation in media. Celebrities in today's world are elevated to the status of idols, and the pervasive message suggests that by emulating their diets, exercise routines and product preferences, one can attain a similar appearance. What many young people are often unaware of is that these celebrities have typically spent hours being meticulously groomed in preparation for professional photoshoots, and their images are subsequently digitally altered and airbrushed to create an illusion of flawlessness.

It is not uncommon for people to spend a lot of time and energy to get the perfect photo to post and then judge themselves on how many likes they receive for it. Images can be lengthened or shortened or slimmed down or enhanced in certain places, blemishes are removed, skin is smoothed out, noses made smaller, muscles are enhanced. Whatever is needed to make an image look "perfect" it can be done on a computer. Children need to be made aware of this. The image that they might see over and over and strive to be like is not even real and it is our responsibility to encourage them to notice.

It might be an idea to show children examples of before-and-after photos to illustrate how images are altered. Encourage them to question the authenticity of images encountered and discuss the potential consequences of striving to achieve unrealistic ideals.

To put a positive spin on this, perhaps introduce them to The Dove Self-Esteem Project and other companies that refuse to use digital manipulation. Dove is committed to making beauty a source of confidence and not anxiety. The Dove project is a global initiative aimed at helping young people develop a positive body image and self-esteem. The project provides educational resources and workshops to parents, teachers and youth leaders, and has reached over 60 million young people worldwide. The project is based on the belief that everyone should feel beautiful regardless of their age, race, size or shape.[28]

Promote Body Diversity

As discussed previously it is pivotal to encourage discussions about body diversity, the danger of internalizing unrealistic ideals, and the importance of accepting that all bodies are worthy no matter their shape or size. As a family, constantly challenge the portrayal of beauty in the media and emphasize that there is no single standard of how a body should look and that a thin body doesn't necessarily mean it is a healthy one. Inspire your children to explore literature on body diversity and, when old enough, to follow accounts that advocate for body diversity and a healthy approach to all sizes.

There are some fantastic resources out there that are created to help children understand that all bodies, no matter shape, or size are equally worthy.

It is crucial to discuss with them that real bodies differ from the Disney princesses and idealized images in the media. Engage them in discussions about respecting people regardless of their size, emphasizing that everyone is unique.

Digital Citizenship

Teach children about responsible online behaviour. Discuss the importance of being respectful and kind to others on social media and in digital communication. Encourage them to report any cyberbullying they encounter and to seek help if they are victims of online harassment.

A Learning Curve For Us All

Navigating the swiftly evolving digital landscape can be a daunting task for parents, yet effective communication remains paramount in educating children about the genuine risks associated with all forms of media. Summing up this chapter it is fundamental to recognize that although we can do our best to guide our children, we can never fully protect them from the dangers of the media.

We can't control aggressive marketing techniques used by the diet and beauty industry. We cannot stop adverts, magazines, cartoons, movies, kids' toys or books from promoting the thin ideal. We cannot stop social media from bombarding us with accounts that promote diet culture.

We can, however, be better role models by promoting responsible media use, advocating for safe and limited media exposure, and fostering an understanding of how all forms of media impact our emotions and behaviours. We can encourage our children to recognize, understand and ignore diet culture advertisements. We can encourage them if they are of age to unfollow or block any accounts that make them feel unworthy or negative about their body.

By nurturing media literacy within the family, we equip our children with the means to critically assess and resist the barrage of messages surrounding body image, diets, digitally enhanced images and all the myths perpetuated by the fashion, diet and beauty industries. We empower our children to become discerning critical thinkers, enabling them to assess the credibility of content effectively. We enable them to navigate the digital landscape safely and confidently, ultimately creating a world where they can grow into resilient and self-assured individuals.

Let us bestow wisdom upon children, teaching them not only to observe but also to question, challenge and critically assess pervasive messages.

9

ENCOURAGING POSITIVE MENTAL HEALTH WITHIN A FAMILY

Within the familial realm, the quest for positive mental health is an ongoing journey. This chapter serves as a compass, guiding us through various steps to help children mature into independent, well-rounded, emotionally resilient and functional adults. In the intricate process of growing up, children absorb not just lessons and knowledge but also the subtle nuances of behaviour, self-perception and emotional expression from the adults around them. Social modelling becomes the canvas upon which they paint their understanding of the world.

Generational patterns repeat when parents mirror how they were parented and act in ways that are familiar. No one sat our parents down with a parenting manual when we were born. Today with easier access to research and the appropriate online platforms there is a plethora of helpful information available. The promising news is that it doesn't matter how far toxic intergenerational patterns go back in your family; what matters is putting an end to them now, and *Breaking the Cycle* for our children – and their children. We have the power to obliterate patterns of stifled emotions, low self-worth and body loathing. We have the power to start a revolution within our homes.

While on this endeavour, we guide our children to believe in themselves, to follow their dreams and to see their bodies as remarkable and diverse, free from the shackles of societal expectations. We teach them to value themselves and others for who they are rather than how they look. In doing this we give them an extra layer of protection in the prevention of developing an eating disorder.

To shift away from the harmful narrative that we are accustomed to, there are numerous actions we can take:

- Prioritize effective communication within the family
- Role model positive mental and physical health
- Validate children's emotions
- Provide nurturing support, fostering a growth mindset
- Involving children in decision making within the family
- Acknowledging children's strengths and celebrate their achievements
- Engage with activities they enjoy, encouraging them to pursue their passions
- Model self-acceptance and practice gratitude
- Teach healthy coping mechanisms
- Embrace body diversity and teach media literacy

Above all, we must love, accept and respect our children just the way they are, no matter their shape or size.

As we navigate this nuanced terrain, the overarching goal is to create a family environment where mental wellbeing is not only prioritized but actively nurtured. By scrutinizing our roles as parents and caregivers, we can lay the groundwork for creating a resilient, empowered and mentally healthy family dynamic. The primary aim is to raise children who possess self-acceptance and self-worth; with the ability to master their emotions and the social skills essential for confident integration into the world. We hold the responsibility of dismantling the influence of diet culture within the home and fostering body image resilience within our children. This chapter is here to help us figure this out step by step.

Allow All Emotions

Healthy communication within the family is key. Children must feel safe to be able to communicate their emotions freely and without fear. Creating a household where all emotions are welcomed and expressed becomes the cornerstone of nurturing emotionally intelligent and empowered individuals. Letting tantrums unfold, offering empathy and validation is critical. Supporting children and encouraging open and honest communication in times of sadness, worry, anger or excitement is massively important. A safe home environment facilitates a child to share openly without the fear of judgment, buffering the prevention of the development of suppressed emotions which often leads to the use of unhealthy coping mechanisms.

It might be helpful to get your hands on this wonderful book by *Sunday Times* bestselling author Fearne Cotton, *Your Mood Journal: feelings journal for kids*. This journal/book is crafted to assist children in recognizing emotions through visual and artistic means. Fearne explains: "I've created this book to help show that it's okay to feel all emotions."

I also recommend checking out mindfulmazingshop.com for a wonderful array of resources to help children get in touch with their emotions.

Throughout my experience of assisting individuals in support groups and online, it has become evident that many people grappling with eating disorders were raised in families that discouraged the open expression of emotions. This environment propelled them to find solace in dangerous alternative coping mechanisms, with food and weight obsessions becoming a common outlet.

In therapy, I unearthed copious amounts of stifled emotions from throughout my life: attempts to express sadness were countered with calls to cheer up, anger was consistently silenced, and moments of excitement were met with requests to calm down. This suppression of my emotions undoubtedly eroded my self-trust, instilling fear and casting doubt upon my own perceptions. Consequently, I sought refuge in food and fixated on my weight as channels for self-expression. It wasn't until I reached my twenties, while undergoing therapy, that I grappled with the profound extent of my emotional disconnection, recognizing that digging up suppressed emotions was essential in order to cultivate emotional awareness and to allow me to fully heal.

Have Difficult Conversations

Encourage open and honest age-appropriate discussions with children, even when addressing difficult topics. Children are often perceptive to family dynamics and global events, so it's important not to shy away from discussing them. Whether it's a family member's illness, a loss or a natural disaster, approach these subjects with transparency and sensitivity. Shielding children from real-life situations doesn't foster resilience; instead, it's essential to involve them in these conversations as part of their journey toward self-discovery. By engaging them in such discussions, we equip them with the tools to navigate challenges and develop into strong, adaptable individuals.

Encourage Active Listening

To nurture a child's self-esteem, it's essential to authentically engage with them and demonstrate a sincere interest in their thoughts and emotions. Meeting them at their level is key – even when discussing topics that may not captivate you! Try to connect by feigning interest, actively listening to their narratives and noting their passions and disinterests. Show curiosity about their school life, friendships and hobbies, ensuring they feel valued and significant. This communicates that their voice matters, bolstering their self-worth and self-confidence. Creating an atmosphere of genuine interest and empathy while refraining from criticism cultivates an environment where their viewpoints are honoured, reinforcing feelings of worthiness. Conversely, criticism or dismissal can be detrimental to self-esteem and self-worth, a factor often linked to eating disorders.

Engage In Activities As a Family

Participating in enjoyable family activities serves as more than just a means of bonding and creating cherished memories – it also fosters an atmosphere of open communication conducive to mental wellbeing. Go for activities tailored to your child's interests. Whether it's sharing meals, immersing in nature, playing sports or embarking on adventures, these experiences facilitate meaningful exchanges and strengthen family connections. By fostering communication in a relaxed and enjoyable setting, these activities encourage children to express themselves freely, ultimately contributing to their overall mental health and happiness, and will help you all develop a strong family bond.

Practise Self-Care

Modelling self-care behaviours to children is essential as it teaches them the value of prioritizing their own wellbeing. When children witness adults engaging in self-care practices such as setting boundaries, taking breaks and engaging in activities that recharge their energy, they learn that self-care is not only acceptable but necessary. It normalizes these behaviours and communicates that it's okay to prioritize one's mental, emotional and physical health.

Additionally, seeing adults take care of themselves serves as a powerful example for children to emulate, fostering the development of healthy habits that they can carry into adulthood.

Ultimately, demonstrating the importance of self-care in our own lives sends a positive and powerful message to our children, equipping them with the tools and mindset to prioritize their own wellbeing and cultivate a lifelong practice of self-care.

Encourage and Support Children's Unique Qualities

Empower your child's self-belief by nurturing their curiosity about their interests, dreams and aspirations. Guide them in discovering their strengths and passions, emphasizing the significance of their individuality. Teach them that it's perfectly acceptable to diverge from the norm and pursue their own path, even if it differs from their peers. Not everyone will be good at maths, not everyone has musical talents or is good at sport. Guide them to recognize their distinctive talents and to understand that not everyone excels in the same areas. This instils in them the value of embracing their uniqueness and helps them realize that it is okay to be different from others. Encourage them to celebrate their personal qualities and remind them that true fulfilment comes from being authentic to themselves, rather than conforming to external expectations.

Encourage the Use of Positive Affirmations

Introducing children to the practice of positive affirmations can be profoundly beneficial for nurturing their self-confidence, self-image and self-belief. By regularly engaging in affirmations that emphasize their strengths, abilities and worth, children develop a more resilient and positive mindset.

The use of affirmations helps to counter negative self-talk and fosters a sense of self-empowerment, enabling children to navigate challenges with greater ease and optimism. Moreover, cultivating a habit of positive self-affirmation from a young age instils a strong foundation of self-esteem and self-worth, which can have lasting effects into adulthood. It teaches children to value themselves and their abilities, leading to healthier relationships, improved mental wellbeing, and a more optimistic outlook on life. Integrating positive affirmations into a child's daily routine can be a powerful tool for fostering their overall emotional and psychological growth.

There is a wonderful set of body-image specific affirmations available from Body Happy Org CIC, a social enterprise promoting positive body image in children. LSW London, a wellbeing stationery company offer a beautiful set of *Kids' Edition Mind* cards. The idea being that children select a card at random every day to encourage patience, resilience and self-love.

Boundaries at Home

Creating a nurturing environment for your child's upbringing is paramount, where healthy boundaries are established and respected. Implement rules that are rational, consistent and fair, ensuring your child comprehends their purpose. Clearly articulate these guidelines and encourage open discussion, allowing your child to voice their perspectives. Be receptive to feedback and apologize when necessary, fostering mutual respect. Additionally, honour their boundaries by respecting their possessions and privacy.

Assigning chores instils a sense of responsibility and importance; celebrate their contributions and offer praise accordingly. Transform household tasks into enjoyable activities, such as tidying toys or assisting with cooking, to instil a sense of responsibility while fostering a positive atmosphere at home. Give them choices and let them make age-appropriate decisions – this gives them a sense of importance, responsibility and independence.

Practise Gratitude

Practising gratitude is scientifically proven to improve physical and psychological health. It is said to improve nervous system regulation, brain health, sleep, heart function, hormone balance, your digestive and immune systems and inflammation. It reduces toxic emotions like guilt, envy and frustration. Leading gratitude researcher Robert A Emmons PhD has found that gratitude increases happiness, reduces depression, enhances empathy and reduces aggression.[29] A regular gratitude practice is also said to increase mental strength, reduce stress and foster resilience.

An engaging activity to promote gratitude involves creating a poster or list where children can jot down five things they're thankful for. Encourage them to reflect on these blessings each night before bed. Make it a daily ritual. Use this opportunity to educate them about the privileges they enjoy, such as access to clean water, education and healthcare, which others may lack. By recognizing these privileges, children learn not to take them for granted.

Additionally, encourage children to create personal gratitude lists, acknowledging the people, possessions and experiences that bring them joy and fulfilment. This practice fosters a sense of appreciation and mindfulness, enriching their perspective on life.

Getting children to practise gratitude for what they already have is such a good habit to get into. Studies show that by being appreciative and thankful can increase our happiness.

You may also wish to practise body gratitude with them. Ask them why they are grateful for – their eyes, their legs, their internal organs. Unless we point out the things to be grateful for children often go through life unaware.

Encourage Mindfulness Activities

In today's fast-paced world, introducing children to mindfulness can be profoundly beneficial for their mental health. With the constant stimulation and pressures of modern life, children often face stress, anxiety and difficulty managing their emotions. Mindfulness activities, such as yoga, meditation, visualization, arts and crafts or anything that encourages them to be present in the moment, provide invaluable tools for navigating these challenges.

By teaching children to cultivate awareness of their thoughts, feelings and surroundings, mindfulness empowers them to regulate their emotions, reduce stress and enhance their overall wellbeing. Moreover, mindfulness fosters resilience, helping children develop the ability to cope with adversity and bounce back from setbacks. By incorporating mindfulness practices into their daily lives, we equip children with lifelong skills to navigate the complexities of the modern world with greater calm, clarity and compassion.

Teach Media Literacy

In the previous chapter, I emphasized the importance of educating children about the pervasive influence of advertising giants in this digital age. It's essential to instil in them a critical awareness that not everything portrayed online or in media is genuine. Encourage curiosity and teach them to question the motives behind advertisements – who benefits and who may be exploited? Educate them about digital manipulation and the prevalence of edited images. Establish clear guidelines for screentime and serve as a role model in adhering to these rules. Foster a culture of critical thinking, particularly regarding messages related to diet culture, prompting them to analyse and understand who stands to gain from such messaging.

Celebrate Body Diversity

Encouraging children to embrace body diversity and cultivate respect for individuals of all shapes and sizes is crucial in buffering against the development of body image problems and struggles with food. In a society inundated with unrealistic beauty standards, children are often bombarded with messages that equate worth with a particular body type. By promoting the acceptance of diverse bodies and emphasizing that everybody deserves love and respect, we instil in children the confidence to embrace their own unique attributes and to appreciate the diversity around them. This inclusive mindset not only fosters positive self-esteem and body image but also helps to mitigate the risk factors associated with the development of eating disorders. By celebrating diversity and promoting body acceptance, we empower children to cultivate a healthy relationship with their bodies and to prioritize overall wellbeing over unrealistic ideals of beauty.

Accept Your Child!

We should wholeheartedly accept our children just as they are for numerous compelling reasons. The size or shape of their body should be of zero importance.

Embracing their unique physical attributes fosters a sense of unconditional love and support, nurturing their self-esteem and self-worth. By accepting them unconditionally, we instil in them the confidence to navigate the world with assurance and resilience. It sends a powerful message that their value lies not in their appearance, but in their character, talents and individuality.

Ultimately, accepting our children builds a foundation of love and belonging, essential for their emotional wellbeing and overall development. This quote by trauma specialist Dr Gabor Mate truly resonates:

"Unconditional parental love is the indispensable nutrient for the child's healthy emotional growth."[30]

Reject Diet Culture at All Costs!

Throughout this book, a recurring theme has been how diet culture perpetuates harmful beliefs surrounding body image, weight and food. From start to finish, the narrative has underscored the importance of understanding diet culture's insidious nature and how to challenge it for the sake of our children. Each chapter has woven together discussions on diet culture and how it influences all our lives. We have learned how to recognize its cunning ways, how to dismantle harmful messaging within our homes, how to promote body diversity and how to help children develop a healthy and balanced approach to food.

Rejecting diet culture within the home is like giving your child a vaccination. It doesn't mean they won't develop an eating disorder. It is, however, critical for safeguarding their mental health and gives them an added layer of protection against the development of food- or body-related struggles.

HOW TO DITCH DIET CULTURE

I've compiled a succinct list outlining what to do and what to avoid to actively combat diet culture within the household.

DON'T

- Diet, or even mention the word "diet" EVER
- Talk about calories

- Weigh yourself
- Comment on bodies – not yours, not your child's, not anyone's
- Label foods as good or bad
- Put your child on a diet EVER
- Suggest that your child should lose weight
- Weigh your child
- Talk about your weight, your child's weight, or anyone else's
- Comment on how little or how much food they are eating
- Fuss over food
- Leave trashy magazines lying around

DO

- Get rid of bathroom scales
- Allow all foods
- Celebrate all bodies
- Accept your body (if this is too difficult, fake it)
- Treat your body with respect
- Model the behaviour you want to see in your children
- Accept and adore your child regardless of their shape or size
- Educate yourself on the insidious nature of diet culture
- Unpack your own fat phobia
- Focus on a person's qualities rather than their appearance
- Challenge people who talk about diet culture in front of your child
- Have age-appropriate conversations about diet-culture
- Be a rebel and *like your body* – the most radical act of the modern age!

When we create a diet-culture-free environment within the home it means that our children exist just a little bit longer unaware of the importance the size and shape of their body holds in the world. When we stop being a pawn in this game our children learn that they are more than a body or an ornament to be admired or ogled. When we stop being a slave to the scale, we teach children that we are more than an arbitrary number. By embodying self-acceptance and a healthy relationship with both body and mind, we lay the foundation for raising resilient, well-rounded individuals. We contribute to breaking the generational cycles of dieting, body loathing, low self-esteem and eating disorders. All children deserve to live a life free from body insecurities and food fears.

A Bright Future

As you embark on this adventure with your family it might be helpful to keep this quote nearby:

> *"Children have never been very good at listening to their elders, but they have never failed to imitate them."*
> *James Baldwin, American writer and civil rights activist*[31]

This venture is about more than just breaking the intergenerational cycle of dieting and body loathing within our family – it is testament to our commitment to nurturing positive mental health overall. By rejecting harmful societal norms and embracing self-acceptance and self-care we foster a culture of compassion, resilience and wellbeing. We are learning to communicate openly, to celebrate our unique bodies, and to find joy in the simple act of nourishing ourselves, both physically and emotionally.

Together, we can pave the way toward a future where our family thrives in body, mind and spirit. This isn't the end of the story, but a new beginning. We are still learning, still growing, but we face the future together, armed with the knowledge that we are worthy of love and acceptance, exactly as we are and may we inspire others to also embark on this path, *Breaking the Cycle*.

FINAL WORDS

My commitment to breaking the cycle of body hatred and food struggles within families is more than a mission; it's a lifelong dedication. I care deeply that countless individuals are denied the joy of life due to an obsessive focus on their body size and food. It pains me to see children succumbing to the same damaging patterns. Every day, I raise my voice on my Instagram and X accounts, advocating for awareness and change. My goal is nothing short of initiating a revolution within homes, empowering adults and instilling hope that positive transformation is possible.

Raising my own daughter in a society fixated on weight and food, I can attest that it is difficult yet possible to break free from this cycle. I firmly believe that every adult has the capacity to set children off on a more positive path.

While I recognize that tackling diet culture and challenging a society that idealizes thinness is a monumental task, there are numerous actions we can take to steer the next generation away from the dark road of diet cycles, food obsessions, body insecurities and eating disorders. By being mindful of our words, actions and treatment of children, we wield the power to offer them a better chance at a life unburdened by food rules and body insecurities.

The idea of my seven-year-old niece – this wonderfully funny, vibrant and hilariously confident girl – expressing hatred toward her body or contemplating going on a diet is something I cannot bear to imagine for even a second. The thought of her feeling "too big", reminiscent of my own struggles at that age, is unbearable. Imagining her in gym class, burdened by self-consciousness about her body and fearing judgment from her peers, is too distressing. I cannot tolerate the idea that she might deny herself a slice of cake at a friend's birthday party out of fear of consequences. My sincere wish is to shield her for as long as possible from the relentless barrage of messages from the outside world and for her to have a positive relationship with food and her body.

Throughout the book we have been made aware of the omnipresence of the messages from the diet and beauty industries and explored how they massively influence how we feel about ourselves. The good news is that even if you still suffer from a negative body image, have a history of dieting behaviour, or have a full-blown eating disorder it does not in any way mean that your children are destined to also follow this path. They do not have to inherit your issues. As you work on healing your own relationship with food and your body you can make your home a body-positive, diet-free and safe environment for the whole family.

To conclude my thoughts, it's essential to acknowledge that there's no absolute guarantee that your child won't be drawn into the cycle of dieting and body negativity. However, it's worth exploring the numerous strategies suggested throughout this book if our shared goal is to avoid setting the stage for the development of an eating disorder. Why not give them an added layer of protection? Why not lessen the risk?

Within our homes, we possess the influence to guide children toward establishing a healthy, positive and enduring relationship with food – one centred on freedom, joy, variety, fun and nourishment, and to allow them to appreciate their bodies and all they contribute. We can pave the way for a happier generation that values their bodies for what they can *do* rather than how they *appear*. The groundwork for cultivating a positive body image begins at home, and our collective efforts can make a substantial difference.

I extend my heartfelt appreciation to those who have stood by me and served as a source of inspiration throughout this voyage, particularly those who participated in support groups over the years and courageously shared their stories.

It is my sincerest desire that readers discover both hope and insight within these pages.

I'd like to wrap up the book with a quote from my 31-year-old daughter, Maria, demonstrating that breaking the cycle within a family is indeed achievable.

"I am so lucky to have a mum who protected me from diet culture as much as she could. I saw how it would have been so easy for me to fall into the trap of wanting and desiring the 'perfect' body, constantly judging my body and other people's bodies, or feeling guilty for not going to the gym or for eating foods that are considered 'junk' or 'bad' or 'fattening'.

"My mum taught me to accept and appreciate my body and she allowed all foods in our home. We did not own bathroom scales and I only learned when I was older that they were banned. I never really knew about diets; I wasn't exposed to diet chat in my home and people's bodies were never judged or commented on. This was my normal when I was little. As I grew older it was hard to avoid 'diet culture'. At high school it was often the topic of conversation – who has gained too much weight? Or what celebrity was the skinniest and had the most amazing body?

"I will be honest and say this type of chat bored me. I wasn't as interested as other girls my age, but I still got involved so as not to be the odd one out. If I went home and mentioned someone's body or weight in front of my mum, she would very quickly challenge me. She encouraged me to think differently and not to judge people by their shape or size. She made me very aware from my early teenage years that people are more than their bodies and that size doesn't matter. I would confide in my mum if I had any

body hang ups. She would be gentle and talk me through them. To help me, she introduced me to body diversity and body positivity. She taught me that gaining weight was okay – as was losing weight – and to just trust that my body was exactly the way it was meant to be. She instilled in me that body changes throughout my life were normal. She would get me to voice what I did love about my body, what I was grateful and ultimately to appreciate the body I have and what it did for me.

"Now as an adult, I see how diet culture and eating disorders are consuming lives, and I couldn't be more grateful that I allow myself to enjoy all foods. I never restrict or feel guilty for what I eat. I know that it is okay for my body to change, that it's okay to put weight on and it's okay to lose weight, as long as I feel good and I am happy. I have never been on a diet in my life. I've rarely weighed myself over the course of my life – only a handful of times out of mere curiosity whenever scales happened to be present in the bathrooms I found myself in. I eat what I want, when I want, and I move my body in ways that are fun. I love going to the gym. I enjoy yoga and often go cycling.

"In September of 2023, I learned that I was expecting a baby. My daughter is due to arrive in May, and throughout these past six months, I've embraced every change my body has undergone with confidence and gratitude. Rather than feeling anxious about these transformations, I've felt a deep sense of pride in what my body is capable of. As I await the arrival of my daughter, one of my priorities as a parent is shielding her from the harmful influences of diet culture. My aim is to nurture a daughter who is not only comfortable in her own skin but also values her worth beyond superficial standards. Though I understand the magnitude of this endeavour, I am committed to doing everything in my power to raise a resilient and body confident young woman."

ACKNOWLEDGEMENTS

I wish to express my heartfelt gratitude to Marion Davies. I am thankful to you every day of my life. You believed in me, and without you, nothing would have been possible. Thank you, Ena Magon, forgiving me the confidence to believe that this book was worth persevering with. Your encouragement and motivation kept me going when it all seemed too overwhelming. Dr. Triona McInerney, without your dedication and expertise, I wouldn't have been able to facilitate the support groups, so a huge thank you. I must express gratitude to everyone who attended our groups over the years, whether at Strathclyde University, Glasgow University, The Tom Allen Centre, or when we went online in 2020. I will always be in awe of your courage, bravery, and honesty. Your experiences live with me, and without your attendance, this book would not have been possible. Thank you to those who bravely shared their personal stories of growing up immersed in diet culture; I have changed names to protect your identities. A final heartfelt thank you to my two rocks, Gary and Maria. You believed in me when I didn't. You both mean the world to me.

USEFUL RESOURCES

Recommended Resources

Crabbe, Megan Jane, *Body Positive Power: How to stop dieting, make peace with your body and live*

Carey, Tanith, *Girls Uninterrupted: Steps for Building Stronger Girls in a Challenging World*

Darpinian, Signe, Sterling, Wendy, Aggarwal, Shelley, *Raising Body Positive Teens: A Parent's Guide to Diet-Free Living, Exercise, and Body Image*

Dixon, Monica, M.S., R.D, *Love the Body You Were Born With: A ten-step workbook for women*

Doyle, Glennon, *untamed: stop pleasing, start living*

Dooner, Caroline, *The F*ck It Diet: Eating Should Be Easy*

Forbes, Molly, *Body Happy Kids: How to Help Children and Teens Love the Skin They're In*

Harrison, Christy, *Anti-Diet: Reclaim Your Time, Money, Well-Being and Happiness Through INTUITIVE EATING*

Hutchinson, Nicky, Calland Chris, *Body Image in the Primary School*

Johnston, Anita PhD, *Eating in the Light of the Moon: how women can transform their relationships with food through myths, metaphors & storytelling*

Kite, Lexie and Lindsay, *More Than a Body: Your Body Is an Instrument, Not an Ornament*

Lewis, Dr Vivienne, *No Body's Perfect: A helper's guide to promoting positive body image in children and young people*

Markey, Charlotte, *The Body Image Book for Girls and The Body Image Book for Boys*

Orbach, Susie, *Fat is a Feminist Issue*

Poppink, Joanna, *Healing Your Hungry Heart*

Reach, Elyse and Tribole, Evelyn, *Intuitive Eating*

Róisín Fariha, *Being in Your Body: A Journal for Self-Love and Body Positivity*

Richardson, Brenda, Lane, Rehr, Elane, *101 Ways to Help Your Daughter Love Her Body*

Scritchfield, Rebecca, *Body Kindness: Transform Your Health from the Inside Out-and Never Say Diet Again*

Sole-Smith, Virginia, *The Eating Instinct*

Wolf, Naomi, *The Beauty Myth*

Reccommended Reading for Children/Teens

Cotton, Fearne, *Your Mood Journal: Activities to Help You Figure out Your Feelings*

Eidens, Alexandra, *Big Life Journal for Children*

Engel, Christiane, *ABC Mindful Me*

Kay, Katty, Shipman, Claire, *The Confidence Code for Girls: Taking risks, messing up, & becoming your amazingly imperfect, totally powerful self*

Markey, Charlotte, *The Body Image Book for Girls: Love Yourself and Grow Up Fearless*

Morgan, Nicola, *Body Brilliant: A Teenage Guide to a Positive Body Image*

Sanders Jessica, *Love Your Body*

Parr, Todd, *It's Okay to Be Different*

Taylor, Renee, Sonya, *Celebrate Your Body: The Ultimate Puberty Book for Girls*

Recommended Resources

mindfulmazingshop.com
www.biglifejournal.com
https://www.dove.com/us/en/dove-self-esteem-project.html
https://www.bodyhappyorg.com/
https://lswmindcards.com/products/lsw-mind-cards
Kay, Katty, Shipman, Claire, *The Confidence Code for Girls
Journal: A Guide to Embracing Your Amazingly Imperfect,
Totally Powerful Self*

Anti-Diet Instagram Accounts to Follow

@moreloveorg
@bodyhappyorg
@anti.diet.kids
@nicolecruzrd
@momgenesthepodcast
@christina_runstheworld
@oona_hanson
@char_markey
@drmorganfrancis
@beauty_redefined
@mollybcounseling
@bodyimagewithbri
@wholistic_health_and_wellness
@embodiedpsychotherapist
@diets_don't_work_haes1
@eatingdisordertherapyla
@elyseresch
@mysignaturenutrition
@food_freedom_coach
@sunnysideupnutritionists
@meganjaynecrabbe

@drchuks_
@priya_tew
@caralisette
@_natashadevon
@recovrywarriors
@v_solesmith
@crystaltalkarges
@chr1styharrisson
@iamchrissyking
@evelyntribole
@dranitajohnston
@drannacolton

REFERENCES

1 https://www.england.nhs.uk/2022/03/nhs-treating-record-number-of-young-people-for-eating-disorder
2 Anti Diet, Christy Harrison, Yellow Kite, 2019, page 49
3 *Body Image in The Primary School*, Nicky Hutchinson and Chris Calland, Routledge, 2011, page 13.
4 https://www.goodreads.com/quotes/597503-the-way-we-talk-to-our-children-becomes-their-inner
5 http://news.bbc.co.uk/1/hi/health/4319105.stm
6 https://www.facebook.com/share/RKBBsD5eon2xR95K/?mibextid=WC7FNe
7 https://www.instagram.com/p/B_g7OHTFOVG/?igsh=MWt5a2VsdGpkdm1hMw==
8 https://www.instagram.com/p/CalUwdRs3im/?igsh=YXU3dmo3dmlwMHgz
9 https://www.facebook.com/share/p/9Vj5uPKHpRFeQU7j/?mibextid=WC7FNe
10 https://www.instagram.com/p/BhhMeZgFalT/?igsh=MXNhcW11b2Y1dGRucA==
11 https://www.girlguiding.org.uk/globalassets/docs-and-resources/research-and-campaigns/girls-attitudes-survey-2016.pdf
12 Crabbe, Megan Jayne, *Body Positive Power*, Penguin Random House UK, 2017, page 6
13 https://www.instagram.com/p/BhhMeZgFalT/?igsh=MXNhcW11b2Y1dGRucA==
14 untamed. stop pleasing, start living, Doyle, Glennon, Penguin Random House UK, 2020, page 216

15 Fragile, The true story of my anorexia, Grahame, Nikki, John Blake Publishing, 2012, pages 9 and 10

16 Family members and peers' negative and positive body talk: How they relate to adolescent girls' body talk and eating disorder attitudes, Body Image, Volume 40, March 2022, pages 213–224 Barbeau, Kheana, Carbonneau Noémie, Pelletier, Luc https://www.sciencedirect.com/science/article/abs/pii/S1740144521001613

17 Family weight talk and dieting: how much do they matter for body dissatisfaction and disordered eating behaviors in adolescent girls? Neumark-Sztainer, Dianne, Bauer, W, Katherine, Friend, Sarah, Hannan, J, Peter, Story, Mary, Berge, M, Jerica https://pubmed.ncbi.nlm.nih.gov/20708566/

18 National Eating Disorders Association, Weight Stigma, Edwards-Gayfield, Paula, MA, LCMHCS, LPC, NCC, CEDS-C, October 2023 https://www.nationaleatingdisorders.org/weight-stigma/#:~:text=Weight%20bias%20can%20increase%20body,the%20sociocultural%20idealization%20of%20thinness.

19 British Journal of Clinical Psychology (1998), 37, 3–13 0 1998 Mothers, daughters and dieting: Investigating the transmission of weight control Andrew J. Hill* and Julie A. Franklin

20 Pike, M, Kathleen, Rodin Judith, Mothers, Daughters, and Disordered Eating, June 1991, Journal of Abnormal Psychology 100(2):198–204 https://www.researchgate.net/publication/21114784_Mothers_Daughters_and_Disordered_Eating Pike, K.M., Rodin, J. 1991

21 Birch, L, Leann, PhD, Abramovitz, Ms, Beth, A, October 2000, J Am Diet Assoc. Five-year-old girls' ideas about dieting are predicted by their mothers' dieting https://www.ncbi.nlm.nih.gov/pmc/articles/PMC2530935/#:~:text=Compared%20to%20girls%20

whose%20mothers,concepts%2C%20and%20beliefs%20
about%20dieting

22 https://ashleihumpert.wordpress.com/2015/02/16/
as-a-child-i-never-heard-one-woman-say-to-me-i-love-
my-body-not-my-mother-my-elder-sister-my-best-friend-
no-one-woman-has-ever-said-i-am-so-proud-of-my-body-
so-i-make-sure-to-say-it-to-my-d/

23 untamed. stop pleasing, start living, Doyle, Glennon,
Penguin Random House UK, 2020, page 216

24 https://www.psychiatry.org/news-room/apa-blogs/eating-
disorders-weight-shaming-and-clean-eating

25 https://www.instagram.com/share/BBO2JlwEvZ

26 https://mind.family/quotes/speak-to-your-children/

27 https://www.girlguiding.org.uk/globalassets/docs-
and-resources/research-and-campaigns/girls-attitudes-
survey-2023.pdf

28 https://www.dove.com/uk/dove-self-esteem-project.html

29 https://www.forbes.com/sites/amymorin/2014/11/23/7-
scientifically-proven-benefits-of-gratitude-that-will-
motivate-you-to-give-thanks-year-round/

30 https://images.app.goo.gl/FpZWeMVKmpUZKYsM6

31 https://www.azquotes.com/author/829-James_A_
Baldwin/tag/children

ABOUT CHERISH EDITIONS

Cherish Editions is a bespoke publishing service for authors of mental health, wellbeing and inspirational books.

As a division of Trigger Publishing, the UK's leading independent mental health and wellbeing publisher, we are experienced in creating and selling positive, responsible, important and inspirational books, which work to de-stigmatize the issues around mental health and improve the mental health and wellbeing of those who read our titles.

Founded by Adam Shaw, a mental health advocate, author and philanthropist, and leading psychologist Lauren Callaghan, Cherish Editions aims to publish books that provide advice, support and inspiration. We nurture our authors so that their stories can unfurl on the page, helping them to share their uplifting and moving stories.

Cherish Editions is unique in that a percentage of the profits from the sale of our books goes directly to leading mental health charity Shawmind, to deliver its vision to provide support for those experiencing mental ill health.

Find out more about Cherish Editions by visiting cherisheditions.com or joining us on:
Twitter @cherisheditions
Facebook @cherisheditions
Instagram @cherisheditions

Cherish
EDITIONS

ABOUT SHAWMIND

A proportion of profits from the sale of all Trigger books go to their sister charity, Shawmind, also founded by Adam Shaw and Lauren Callaghan. The charity aims to ensure that everyone has access to mental health resources whenever they need them.

Find out more about the work Shawmind do by visiting shawmind.org or joining them on:
  Twitter @Shawmind_
  Facebook @ShawmindUK
  Instagram @Shawmind_

Your Local Mental Health & Wellbeing Charity

www.ingramcontent.com/pod-product-compliance
Ingram Content Group UK Ltd.
Pitfield, Milton Keynes, MK11 3LW, UK
UKHW020353260425
457838UK00009BA/22